A QUESTION OF DUTY

A Question Of Duty

The Curragh Incident 1914

Paul O'Brien

NEW ISLAND

A QUESTION OF DUTY
First published 2014
by New Island
2 Brookside
Dundrum Road
Dublin 14
www.newisland.ie

PRINT ISBN: 978-1-84840-314-7
EPUB ISBN: 978-1-84840-315-4
MOBI ISBN: 978-1-84840-316-1

British Library Cataloguing Data. A CIP catalogue record for this book is available from the British Library

Typeset by JM InfoTech INDIA
Cover design by Anna Shcherbakova.
Printed by ScandBook AB, Sweden

10 9 8 7 6 5 4 3 2 1

Just because you do not take an interest in politics doesn't mean politics won't take an interest in you.

Pericles, 430 BC

Contents

Prologue

On 28 June 1914, Gavrilo Princip, a 19-year-old Serbian nationalist, waited patiently for the Archduke Franz Ferdinand, heir to the Austro-Hungarian Empire, to arrive on an official visit to Sarajevo, the capital city of Bosnia. The Archduke's car drove through the narrow streets until, after taking a wrong turn, it stalled. As the driver attempted to restart the vehicle, Princip stepped forward from the crowd, produced a 9mm Browning semi automatic pistol and fired three shots. Franz Ferdinand was struck in the neck. His wife Sophie, who was pregnant with their fourth child, took a bullet to the stomach. Both were soon declared dead.

While the assassination of the Archduke Ferdinand by an extreme Serbian organisation known as the Black Hand was not the sole or principal cause of the events that followed, it was seen by many as the lighting of the fuse that set Europe ablaze. As the sabre-rattling of the world's politicians increased, the world's armies mobilised and made ready for war. World War I or the Great War, as it was to become known, had commenced.

England expects that every man will do his duty.[1]

Britain, like many other European countries at that time, relied on the fact that every civilian was in fact a citizen soldier. Motivated by feelings of patriotism, they were fighting for the society to which they belonged. Like soldiers, they had a moral and legal obligation to obey the lawful orders of their officers and leaders.

As the armies of the world prepared for war, British and Irish politicians heaved a sigh of relief. Unknown to many people, a major civil war in Britain and Ireland had just been averted. The Protestant population of Ireland, which constituted a local majority in the province of Ulster in the north-east, believed that their economic prosperity arose from Ireland's union with Britain. Fearing domination by an Irish Catholic parliament, they prepared to oppose Home Rule. Ulster Unionists had armed themselves in preparation to defend the union with Britain.

The threat of armed conflict in Ireland once again came to the fore as British troops were put on alert for a possible march on Ulster. In response, Brigadier General Hubert Gough and officers of the 3rd Cavalry Brigade stationed at the Curragh Army Camp threatened to resign rather than deploy their forces in any attempt to coerce Ulster into accepting Home Rule.

This was the so called Curragh Mutiny, which precipitated the most serious crisis of civil-military relations in modern British history. It is historically significant as it was one of the

---

1 The signal sent by Admiral Horatio Nelson from his flagship HMS Victory as the Battle of Trafalgar was about to commence on 21 October 1805. *The Oxford Dictionary of Quotations* (Oxford University Press, Oxford, 1979) p. 360.

few times in modern history that the British army rebelled against a government. The history of Ireland has many 'what ifs' and the Curragh Incident, as it was to become known, is one of those.

This complicated affair poses a number of questions for those interested in British and Irish military history. What were the events that led a government to issue a declaration of military mobilisation against its own subjects? The British government's reaction to the escalating situation and the divisions within the ranks of the military must also be examined. The press lambasted the Liberal government and the military by referring to events at the Curragh as a mutiny. What constitutes a mutiny, and can the incident at the Curragh be deemed such? Officers and men that refuse an order given by a superior may face charges of insubordination, a very serious charge that can result in a court martial and imprisonment. In a war situation it can also result in execution.

The events at the Curragh greatly weakened the relationship between the British government and its army, an army that in 1914 was undersized and under-resourced. A question that is often overlooked is did the events at the Curragh Camp have any effect on the army's morale and its ability to fight in the Great War?

In Ireland, many in the Nationalist community had lost all confidence in parliamentary procedure. They concluded that if an armed force could be used to oppose Home Rule, a similar force could be used to secure it. The deteriorating political and military situation was causing more and more Nationalists to seek an alternative way to achieve Home Rule. As Patrick Pearse, a founding member of the Irish Volunteers, stated: 'I think the Orangeman with a rifle a much less ridiculous figure than the Nationalist without a rifle.'[2]

An armed Nationalist insurrection in Ireland was seen by many at the time as unavoidable. As in Europe, the fuse had also been lit in Ireland.

---

2   Aldous, R. and Puirséil, N., *We Declare*, Quercus, London, 2008, p. 113.

Introduction

At the beginning of the twentieth century, Ireland formed part of the United Kingdom of Great Britain and Ireland, a connection that shaped the politics and administration of the island.

With its own parliament in Dublin since the thirteenth century, Ireland was once considered a separate kingdom. However, with the implementation of the Act of Union in 1801, Ireland's legal independence changed dramatically. Britain's involvement in the Napoleonic Wars against France between 1792 and 1815 had a detrimental effect on political and social affairs in Ireland.

The rebellion that erupted in Ireland in 1798 meant the British government considered the country a serious security threat. With its main army away fighting in Europe and the total military garrison in Ireland numbering just 12,000 troops, the British administration in Ireland employed the use of local militias to put down the rebellion, which they did with considerable force and brutality.

The British government decided that, to end instability in Ireland, direct rule from the Houses of Parliament in London had to be applied. In 1799, Undersecretary Edward Cooke wrote to Prime Minister William Pitt that, 'The Union is the only means of preventing Ireland from becoming too great and too powerful.'[3]

In 1801, Ireland's legal independence was removed by Westminster with the implementation of the Act of Union. The Irish Parliament passed the Act by 158 votes to 115. For the next hundred years Irish politics would be dominated by attempts to change or destroy that Act of Union.

In the decades that followed the Act, the country was to undergo great social, political, economic and religious changes. Though the majority of the people were Catholic, Protestantism was the established religion of the state. As in the Irish Parliament, Irish Catholics did not have representation in the parliament in London. In 1829, after his success in relation to the granting of Catholic Emancipation, Daniel O'Connell began to call for a repeal of the Act of Union. However, mass meetings and political agitation were not enough to bring about new legislation and O'Connell's campaign soon collapsed.

While the Famine of the 1840s devastated the country, it did not lessen the campaign against the Act of Union. A failed rising in 1848 reminded the establishment that a strong militancy still existed in the country and that elements within Irish society sought an independent parliament.

However it was the rise of the Fenian movement in the 1850s and its subsequent campaigns in Ireland and on the English mainland that proved conclusively that Irish violence was the product of Irish grievance.

The police in Ireland and Britain sought to curtail and stamp out any form of insurgency. Many Fenians were tried

---

3   Parliamentary Papers, House of Commons and Command, 1799.

publicly and faced lengthy prison sentences or transportation. In Ireland, the constabulary were an armed semi-military organisation operating from posts scattered at strategic points throughout the country. While the police in England were housed in 'stations', in Ireland they were housed in 'barracks', a fact that reflected the besieged position of the law in Ireland.

The Fenian violence and heavy-handed policing turned many Irishmen back to the tradition of parliamentary agitation. It also caused English statesmen to reconsider the Irish Question. While the latter part of the nineteenth century would be dominated by colonial affairs, the Irish Question would keep its place in parliamentary discussion. However, while some politicians discussed the matter, others wanted action.

Even though the Irish Question was a dominant topic of discussion in the Houses of Parliament since the implementation of the Act of Union, the Irish were severely disadvantaged in their pursuit of Home Rule. The reason for this was the way in which the political structure of the House of Commons functioned.

The British Parliament consisted, as it still does, of an upper house, the House of Lords, and a lower house, the House of Commons. While the population elected the members of the House of Commons, the members of the House of Lords, the Lords Spiritual and the Lords Temporal, were appointed and had the power to reject and thus defeat bills approved and passed by the Commons. The membership consisted of senior bishops of the Church of England and members of the peerage appointed by the sovereign on the advice of the Prime Minister. Many of those sitting in the House of Lords were the aristocratic and the wealthy; for the most part they supported the Conservatives against the Liberals.

From 1870, a strong Irish nationalist party appeared in Westminster demanding an Irish parliament. By the beginning of 1885, the Irish Parliamentary Party, or the Irish Party as it was often called, led by Charles Stuart Parnell, had managed to convince the Liberal and the Conservative parties that in the coming election either party might need to depend on Irish support if they wanted to stay in government. The subsequent general election in November 1885 resulted in Parnell securing eighty-six seats, which was enough to hold the balance of power between the two main British parties. While Parnell toyed with both sides, William Gladstone, the leader of the Liberal Party, decided to lend his support to Home Rule. In reference to the Act of Union, Gladstone stated:

> *There is no blacker or fouler transaction in the history of man. We used the whole civil government of Ireland as an engine of wholesale corruption ... we obtained that union against the sense of every class of the community by wholesale bribery and unblushing intimidation.*[4]

The year 1885 also saw the emergence in Dublin of Irish unionism. Many people had become concerned by the activities of the Irish Party and believed that the union between Britain and Ireland was under serious threat. Unionism received huge support from the Protestant population in Ulster. The Unionists planned to establish a strong and disciplined opposition movement in the province against Home Rule.

---

4   Jenkins, R., Gladstone: A Biography, Macmillan, London, 2002, p. 185

By February 1886, with the support of the Irish Party, Gladstone was back in Parliament as Prime Minister. The Liberals, anxious to retain Irish support, prompted them to introduce a Home Rule Bill in Parliament on 8 April 1886. This action split the Liberal Party, with the dissenting Liberals, including Joseph Chamberlain, joining the Conservatives in defeating the Bill. Many opposed to Home Rule believed that the establishment of a separate Irish Parliament would destroy the union with Britain and ultimately lead to the break up of the British Empire.

However, this defeat did not deter Gladstone and a second Home Rule Bill was introduced on 13 February 1893. While much of this Bill remained similar to the earlier one, the Bill of 1893 emphasised Westminster's supremacy over any parliament established in Dublin. It also said that foreign affairs, defence, trade and customs would all remain under the control of the Parliament in Westminster. However, the main difference was that Irish members of Parliament would be allowed to continue to sit at Westminster. The Unionists in Westminster objected to the Bill, arguing that Home Rule in any form would not satisfy Irish Nationalists and that it would only serve as the first step on the road to full independence from Britain.

The ranks of the Irish Party were at that time divided in relation to Parnell's personal affairs. While some members supported the Bill, the anti-Parnellites under John Redmond believed that it was nothing more than a provisional settlement.

The second Home Rule Bill was debated for eighty-two days, longer than any other Bill in the nineteenth century. Gladstone and his government defended each clause and it survived its third reading in the House of Commons by 301 votes to 267.

However, on 8 September 1893, the Bill was overwhelmingly rejected in the House of Lords, where 41 peers supported the bill and 419 voted against it.

William Gladstone resigned in March 1894 and was replaced by Lord Rosebery, a staunch imperialist who had no intention of continuing to press for Home Rule for Ireland. As domestic affairs dominated debates in the House of Commons, John Redmond and John Dillon worked tirelessly to re-unite the Irish Party.

Born in County Wexford, John Redmond was appointed leader of the Home Rule Party in 1900. Like Parnell before him, John Redmond knew that his party held the balance of power within the Commons. In relation to Home Rule he wrote:

We do not seek any alternative of [sic.] the constitution or supremacy of the imperial parliament. We ask merely to be permitted to take our place in the ranks of those other portions of the British Empire – some twenty-eight in number – which, in their own purely local affairs, are governed by free representative institutions of their own.[5]

In 1906 the Liberals were returned to power under Henry Campbell-Bannerman, the Prime Minister from 1906 to 1908. The party did not have to depend on the support of the Irish Party for their majority in the House of Commons but this situation changed dramatically with the budget crisis of 1909. The House of Lords' rejection of Chancellor of the

---

5   Redmond, J., 'What Ireland Wants', *McClure's Magazine*, October 1910.

Exchequer David Lloyd George's budget was the culmination of tensions between the two houses since the Liberals had taken office. However there was more at stake than the budget: the Liberals sought to bring to an end the right of the House of Lords to veto legislation that had been passed in the House of Commons. This vetoing action was crucial to the Unionists because Conservatives who had rejected any Home Rule Bill dominated the House of Lords.

This constitutional crisis ended in 1911 with the passing of the Parliament Act. According to this Act, the House of Lords lost its power to veto legislation and could only delay Bills from becoming law for two years, after which time they would automatically pass into law. This meant that the Conservative-dominated House of Lords could no longer act as a bulwark against Home Rule.

The general election of 1910 resulted in the Liberal Party emerging as the largest party but with only two seats more than the Conservatives. The Liberals had therefore lost their overall majority and in order to stay in office they had to depend on the support of the Labour Party and the Irish Party under John Redmond.

Two elections in 1910 resulted in the Redmondite party holding the balance of power in the House of Commons. With the Liberals and the Conservatives in such a precarious situation, Redmond knew how and when to push the Home Rule agenda.

With the Liberal government, now led by Herbert Asquith, anxious for Irish support to stay in office, Home Rule for Ireland had become a question of political arithmetic for the Liberals. Asquith was a very capable politician, having pushed through a number of major constitutional and social reforms, and was confident he could do the same with the Home Rule Bill.

In relation to the question of Home Rule for Ireland, First Lord of the Admiralty Winston Churchill stated in a speech in 1912 that:

It would be a great disaster to Ireland if the Protestant population in the North stood aloof from a National Parliament .... I defy respectfully, and I dialectically defy you, by the utmost exercise of your imagination, to conjure up or picture even any set of circumstances in which the ruin of England would not mean the ruin of Ireland also.... Never before has so little been asked, never before have so many people asked for it.[6]

Churchill was educated at Harrow and Sandhurst and served with the 4th Hussars. After seeing service overseas he entered the Houses of Parliament in 1900. He was considered by many as arrogant, brazen and overconfident and was known as a person who enjoyed war. When Churchill appeared in Belfast to speak at the City Hall, the venue had to be relocated to a tent due the opposition to his presence in the province. Churchill was livid and declared that he had lost all patience with Unionists and the escalating situation in Ulster.

The Home Rule Bill passed its final reading in the House of Commons in 1912, leading many to believe that Home Rule for Ireland was soon to be on the statute books. The Ulster Unionists were left with two alternatives in relation to the Home

---

6   Langworth, R. M. (ed.), *Churchill in his Own Words*, Ebury Press, London, 2012, p.167.

Rule Bill. They could work with the government in relation to the Bill in order to secure special provisions for Ulster or they could adopt an uncompromising position against Home Rule.

Having chosen the latter course of action, the Unionists elected Edward Carson as their leader. Carson was born in Harcourt Street, Dublin in 1854. Educated at Trinity College, he was called to the bar in 1877. Appointed solicitor general for England, Carson was knighted by Queen Victoria in 1900. A staunch Unionist, he objected to Home Rule for Ireland.

In 1911, Carson visited Belfast and met with businessman and parliamentarian, James Craig. The threat of Home Rule had rallied thousands of Unionists and had gained support from many influential businessmen and military officers in the province.

In Parliament, political parties were divided over the possible granting of Home Rule for Ireland. While elements within the Conservative Party supported the Unionists, there were some members who had reservations. Former Conservative Prime Minister, Arthur Balfour, wrote:

I do not agree that Ulstermen are wrong to act as they are acting under existing conditions. Were I in their case, I should probably do as they do. But I most strongly feel that nothing can be more demoralising to a society than that some of its very best and most loyal members should deliberately organise themselves for the purpose of offering (if needed) armed resistance to persons holding the King's commission and representing lawful authority.[7]

7   Arthur Balfour to Andrew Bonar Law, Balfour Papers, Add. Mss 49693, British Library, London, 23 September 1913.

There were, however, those within Parliament who would not only support the Unionists politically but who encouraged militancy. The 'Orange Card', a phrase that was originally coined by Lord Randolph Churchill, father of Winston, was to be played to the full.

In relation to the Unionists, the Conservative leader Andrew Bonar Law stated: 'There will not be wanting help from across the channel when the hour of battle comes.'[8]

That hour of battle was gradually coming closer.

---

8   From speech at Balmoral, April 1912, quoted in Beckett, I. (ed.), *The Army and the Curragh Incident 1914*, The Bodley Head, London, 1986, p. 50.

Chapter 1

Beware the Ides of March

20 MARCH 1914, MORNING

At 09.30 hours on Friday, 20 March 1914, six British army officers walked briskly through the corridors of Army Headquarters in Parkgate Street, Dublin. The officers were part of the Irish Command from the Curragh Army Camp in County Kildare. They had been summoned to Dublin to attend a meeting with Lieutenant General Sir Arthur Paget, general officer commanding the forces in Ireland. As they made their way to the Lieutenant General's office, their footsteps loud on the wooden floors, they ignored the many oil paintings of past commanders that adorned the walls.

Major General Sir Charles Fergusson and his fellow officers Brigadier General S. P. Rolt and Brigadier General Hubert Gough had arrived in Dublin via the 08.15 train from Kildare. Brigadier General G. J. Cuthbert was already waiting for his colleagues along with Major General L. B. Friend and Colonel Hill.

Once the officers entered the Lieutenant General's office, their eyes wandered over the odds and ends of furniture which

11

were littered with paperwork. Over the fireplace hung a portrait of King George V in military uniform.

Lieutenant General Paget strode into the room. The officers thought that his manner was in accordance with his uniform: he was stern and pompous and smoking a cigar. Before the meeting commenced he ordered that no notes were to be taken, a request that surprised all those in attendance.

He announced that 'active operations are about to commence against Ulster.' 'I am not expecting any bloodshed,' he said. 'We are too strong.' He continued: 'The Fleet is in Belfast Harbour and some ships are also in Dublin Bay.'[9] Looking at Brigadier General Gough, Paget exclaimed, 'You need expect no mercy from your old friend in the War Office', by whom he meant Field Marshal Sir John French. Gough was incensed that he had been picked out and threatened.

Paget stated that he had received the following concessions from the War Office in London and that these were final and that no officer should seek assistance from any old friends in the War Office.

Officers actually domiciled in Ulster would be exempted from taking part in any operation that might take place. They would be permitted to 'disappear' (that being the exact phrase used by the War Office) and when all was over would be allowed to resume their places without their careers or positions being affected.

Officers who stated they were unwilling to serve might tender their resignations, but these could not be accepted. Officers doing so would be dismissed from the service.

---

9   Gough, General Sir H., *Soldiering On*, Arthur Baker Ltd, London, 1954, p. 102.

The phrase 'domiciled in Ulster' was to be strictly interpreted as those who actually had their homes within the province. Paget stated that all brigadiers were responsible, under penalty of court martial, to verify the genuineness of any applications submitted by those who were not taking part in operations.

He also stated that any officer who was not willing to take part in this operation must come to a decision and, to that end, they were not to attend any other conferences that day. Paget also ordered that a squadron of cavalry from Dublin was to be held in readiness to march northwards the following day.

The six generals and one colonel sat for a few moments in uncomfortable silence. The atmosphere was tense.

Paget asked if any of the officers had any remarks to make. Gough was the first to speak. He asked if the concession of 'disappearance' could be granted to all Irish officers. Even though he could not claim exemption as a resident of Ulster, Gough stated that he was born in Ireland and would have difficulty taking up arms against Ulster Unionists, many of whom were personal friends. He also asked how the 'disappearance' of officers was to be arranged. Tapping on the table with a pencil to emphasise his words, Paget stated that Gough could not claim exemption and that he must consider his position seriously. He did not answer Gough's second question.

As the meeting broke up Paget reiterated his former warning to Gough: 'You can expect no help from the other side.' Four quick strides took Paget to the door and with a swift movement he threw it open. As the officers filed out the door, Paget said, 'Tell your officers to trust me and there will be no bloodshed.'

As the officers assembled outside, Major General Fergusson suggested that they should discuss the ultimatum that had been put to them and that the 'the army must hold together.' Rolt and Cuthbert agreed with their commander but Gough, unable to find the words to frame the protest that rose to his lips, declared bluntly that he would not go. He was incensed that he was singled out when Paget said that he could 'expect no help from his friends at the War Office'.

The party broke up and the officers left the building. Gough walked briskly from HQ to Marlborough Barracks, where the 5th Lancers were billeted. Before he entered the barracks he stopped at a telegraph office and sent a wire to his brother, John Gough, who was Chief Staff Officer to General Douglas Haig at Aldershot, England. The message read: 'The alternative of marching against Ulster or resigning from the Service [has] just been offered me by Paget. Am accepting second alternative. Do you think I am right?'

On entering Marlborough Barracks he sought Lieutenant Colonel Parker, who had been recently promoted to the command of the 5th Lancers. Parker's reaction to the news was one of indignation. The two officers headed to the officers' mess where they managed to assemble fifteen officers, three quarters of those on duty. Here Gough laid Paget's ultimatum before them, giving them two hours to reach a decision. Within those two hours, the seventeen officers, including the Colonel, decided to accept dismissal from the army rather than take part in active operations against Ulster.

Meanwhile, Fergusson, having left the meeting with Paget earlier in the day, was required to remain in Dublin that afternoon to attend another meeting and used this opportunity to draft a document that he could issue to his unit commanders:

In view of the possibility of active operations in Ulster, the War Office has authorized the following communication to officers:

Officers whose homes are actually in the province of Ulster who wish to do so may apply for permission to be absent from duty during the period of operations, and will be allowed to 'disappear' from Ireland. Such officers will, subsequently, be reinstated, and will suffer no loss in their career.

Any other officer who from conscientious or other motives is not prepared to carry out his duty as ordered, should say so at once. Such officers will at once be dismissed from the service.

As regards (1), the words underlined are to be taken literally and strictly, and Brigadiers and O.C. Units are responsible [under penalty of Court Martial] that only such officers as come under that description are allowed to forward applications to 'disappear'.

As regards (2), it is hoped that very few cases will be found of officers who elect to sever their connection with the service. All decisions must be made at once, and application forwarded to Headquarters 5th Division by this evening if possible.

Charles Fergusson, Major-Genl.

Commanding 5th Division and troops Curragh[10]

Parkgate, Dublin
20th March 1914

---

10 Beckett, *The Army and the Curragh Incident 1914*, p. 81.

Summoning his aide-de-camp, Fergusson gave him the written order and told him in a few words 'what was in the wind'. He was to take the order to the Curragh Camp and issue it to the unit commanders.

In England, Gough's brother John, having received the telegram, contacted the Director of Military Operations Major General Sir Henry Wilson in relation to the escalating situation in Dublin and Kildare. Wilson's immediate response was to counsel calm and with much difficulty persuaded Gough 'not to send in his papers till tomorrow when we must find out if this is all true'. 'We must,' he wrote, 'steady ourselves a bit'.[11] While Wilson counselled the Gough brothers, he realised that the unfolding situation in Ireland could provide a window of opportunity for the right person, an opportunity to cause dissention amongst the ranks of the government and the army.

The irons were in the fire.

---

11 20 March 1914, from Callwell, Major General Sir C. E., *Field Marshall Sir Henry Wilson, His Life and Diaries*, vol. 2, London, Cassell & Co., 1927, p. 209.

Chapter 2

Decisions, Decisions

20 MARCH 1914, AFTERNOON

For centuries, thousands of British troops had been stationed throughout every province in Ireland. In the aftermath of the Act of Union, the threat of foreign invasion, sedition and agrarian unrest continually posed problems for the British administration at Dublin Castle. In 1831 Lord Anglesey stated: 'It is idle and absurd to shut your eyes to the degrading fact. We have positively nothing to look to [in Ireland] but the army.'[12]

One of the first purpose-built barracks in the world was the Royal Barracks in Dublin, which was constructed along the quays of the River Liffey in 1701. This military compound housed infantry and cavalry and was to continually expand in order to house thousands of troops that were needed to garrison the country. The Anglo-French Wars from 1792 to

---

12 Muenger E. A., *The British Military Dilemma in Ireland 1886–1914*, Gill & Macmillan, Dublin, 1991, p. 3.

1815 led to the widespread construction of military barracks throughout England, Scotland, Wales and Ireland. In order to secure Ireland and accommodate potential recruits, the construction of military barracks increased throughout the island and the country was divided into four military districts, each with its own general staff. At this time it was estimated that there were 126,000 troops stationed in Ireland, of whom 46,000 were regulars (cavalry, infantry and artillery), 27,000 militia and 53,000 yeomanry. Battalions were rotated every three years in and out of the country with a central reserve being stationed at Athlone.

During the early nineteenth century numerous training exercises were organised 50km from Dublin City on the plains of the Curragh in County Kildare. The Curragh plains were ideal for exercising men, horses and guns. Thousands of soldiers took part in manoeuvres on the 4,870 acres of grassland, often living under canvas or billeted in specially constructed wooden huts.

It was during the Crimean War (1854–1856) that the idea for a permanent training camp located on the Curragh plains was put forward. Lieutenant Colonel Henry Lugard, Assistant General of the Royal Engineers, states that the Curragh provided a 'means of accommodating a large force of infantry for the purpose of being trained and manoeuvred in conjunction with Cavalry and Artillery…'.[13]

At Army Headquarters in Dublin, Paget received a telegram from the War Office stating that General Macready, the officer who was to take charge of the situation in Ulster, was recovering from a bout of malaria.

---

13   Muenger, *The British Military Dilemma in Ireland 1886–1914*, p. 3.

Sir N. Macready is better, but cannot cross before Sunday.

*It will be essential for you to arrange that some officer repre-
sents him for the moment as Birrel has issued instructions to
Commissioner of Police, Belfast, to take instructions from officer
appointed General Officer Commanding there. Wire name of
officers appointed temporarily as soon as possible.*

*You should apply to Great Northern Railway for facilities for
transport of troops and let me know their reply to-day. This may
give rise to important legal questions.*

*The commanding officers of two cruisers now at Kingstown will
report to you. Inform Admiralty as soon as possible if battalion
intended for Dundalk goes by rail or by sea.*

*Destroyer 'Firedrake' last night left Portland for Kingstown to be
at your disposal.*

*You may think it right to take special measures for the comfort of
your troops owing to the rough weather.*

Any necessary additional expenditure is authorized by this telegram.

Report generally on the situation by wire this afternoon.[14]

After the meeting at HQ with Paget, Brigadier General S.
P. Rolt travelled by motor car to the Curragh and outlined
the ultimatum to his battalion commanders. The Colonels
dispersed and summoned their junior officers in order to relay
the information they had just received. One officer wrote later:
'Everyone objects to going and nine out of ten refuse under

---

14 Beckett, *The Army and the Curragh Incident 1914*, p. 117.

any conditions to go.' Cuthbert's battalions had news of events before noon.

Having finished in Marlborough Barracks, Brigadier General Gough travelled to the Curragh Camp, where he arrived at 15.30 hours. He immediately ordered that all remaining officers of the 16th Lancers, the 4th Hussars, the Horse Artillery, the D and E Batteries under Colonel Breeks, and the Royal Engineers assemble in the officers' mess in Ponsonby Barrracks. Gough laid the ultimatum before his officers and told them each man must decide for himself. He also told them that they had the option of dismissal. He requested that they decide by 17.30 hours. Second Lieutenant W. Scott-Watson wrote to his father:

This evening I and the other officers of our regiment were called upon to make the most momentous decision of our lives. We were all assembled in the Colonel's office, and he read out the following proclamation from the War Office:

In view of the possible active operations in Ulster, all officers <u>domiciled in Ulster</u> will be allowed to disappear from Ireland till the operations are over. Any officer who, from conscientious reasons, refuses to take part in these operations will send in an application by 10 a.m. tomorrow. Any officer doing so will be <u>dismissed from the Service</u>.

This we all agreed is the greatest outrage that has ever been perpetrated on the Service. We have had to make this decision without any opportunity of discussing it with our people.

The words 'domiciled in Ulster' have been underlined, and under penalty of court-martial our Colonel has to state whether a man is domiciled in Ulster or not.

I had hardly time to wire for your opinion, so I have decided to carry on. Seven in my Brigade have decided to refuse, and will probably be dismissed [from] the Service either tomorrow or very shortly.

I have decided to stay for the following reasons:

Although, as you know, my sympathies are absolutely with Ulster, I think that at a time like this the army must stick together. If we once start to disintegrate the Service, then goodbye to the Empire and anything else that matters.

Moreover, in case of strike duty, the men whose sympathies are fairly obviously with the strikers have to carry on and do their duty, so that now it is up to us to do the same.

I hope and pray that I have done the right thing, but anyway it is now too late for anything else, for if you don't avail yourself of this opportunity of quitting, and then later on you want to do so, it means a court-martial, with a possibility of being shot.

Altogether, it is the most diabolically ingenious thing that has ever been brought in. What we especially detest is being dismissed and not allowed to resign.[15]

However, before the meeting broke up, all except two had opted for dismissal.

Paget heard about Gough's visit to Marlborough Barracks and immediately sought Colonel Parker. A heated argument ensued between the two officers in relation to Gough's visit and the result of the ultimatum that Gough had laid before the men. Demanding that the 5th Lancers should reconsider

---

15 Beckett, *The Army and the Curragh Incident 1914*, p. 83.

their decisions, Paget repeated that, without the army, 'Ulster would be in a blaze on Saturday.' He appealed to Parker stating 'that his men might proceed to Ulster and chuck it in when the fighting began'. Shocked, Parker replied: 'That would be deserting our men!' On leaving the barracks, Paget ordered Parker to reconsider and report to him the following morning. He sent a telegram to the War Office, stating:

> *Officer commanding the 5th Lancers states that all officers except two, and one doubtful, are resigning their commissions to-day. I much fear same condition in the 16th Lancers. Fear men will refuse to move.*[16]

As events were unfolding in Dublin and the Curragh Camp, senior British army commander Field Marshal Lord Roberts wrote an urgent letter of warning from his desk at the War Office in London to Prime Minister H. H. A. Asquith:

> *I am unwilling to trouble you with a letter at a time of great political tension, and I certainly would not do so were it not that the matter about which I desire to write to you is one of such vital urgency as to impel me to bring it to your notice without further delay.*

> *The statements made by yourself and your colleagues in Parliament and elsewhere show clearly that you contemplate using the forces of the Crown for the purpose of compelling the Ulster Unionists to submit to Home Rule. Having an intimate knowledge of the Army and being in close touch with British officers in all parts of*

---

16 Beckett, *The Army and the Curragh Incident 1914*, p. 86.

the *Empire*, I have no hesitation in telling you that any attempt of this kind would place an intolerable strain on the discipline of the Army, and would produce within it a state of demoralisation from which it would, in my opinion, never recover.

It is certain that Civil War, or, as you call it, 'Civil Commotion', cannot be confined to Ulster, nor to Ireland, nor to Great Britain. It is also certain we shall have outbreaks of violence in many of our large towns. The effect in India, where the present conditions are full of anxiety, may be incalculable, and it is at least conceivable that some European power might take advantage of our domestic difficulties to say insulting things, or even to push inadmissible claims at a moment when we should be powerless to resist them.

The officers and men of the Army are under no misapprehension as to the gravity of the situation. [T]hey are amongst the most loyal and law-abiding of any of His Majesty's subjects, but they are also intelligent men, and they realise to the full that, no matter under what legal guise the order may be given to them, they may be asked to shoot down fellow countrymen who, like themselves, would be fighting under the Union Jack, and also, like themselves, would go to their death singing 'God Save the King'. And, please remember, as our soldiers will remember, that all this will seem to them to be done at the bidding of men who have never missed an opportunity of slandering and vilifying the Army in the grossest manner.

The officers and men of the Army are not politicians, and never concern themselves with the fate of parties, and this very fact prevents their minds being obscured by Party cries and party tactics, and allows them to see the true state of affairs.

23

So certain am I of what will happen should you make this demand upon the Army, that I entreat you to pause before taking so fatal a step.[17]

If the disenchantment that was evident in the Curragh Camp was allowed to spread, Paget knew that military camps throughout Ireland and England would be in danger of following suit. Years had been spent reforming the armed forces and the Curragh Army Camp in County Kildare was one of the most important training camps in Europe.

Construction of this permanent training camp had commenced in 1855 and it comprised of 10 barrack buildings that could each accommodate 1,000 soldiers. Purpose-built quarters for officers were erected and within a short period of time the facilities were increased in order to billet over 10,000 soldiers. Military engineers designed a camp that incorporated buildings such as a post office, a fire station, two churches, a water pumping station, a clock tower and a courthouse. A new road network linked the camp with a series of rifle ranges and training grounds. The roads also connected the camp to military administrative areas at Newbridge, located two miles to the north-east of the Curragh's edge and six miles from Kildare town. Rail links were also utilised as the Great Southern and Western Railway ran from Dublin to Cork and at the north-west of the Curragh there was a short spur line or siding used for the entraining of troops.

In the years that followed, the Curragh was recognised as one of the best equipped training grounds in the British Isles.

---

17 Beckett, *The Army & the Curragh Incident 1914*, p. 55.

Barracks constructed of red brick soon replaced the original wooden barrack buildings.

In 1881 Joseph Chamberlain stated, 'The [English] system in Ireland is founded on the bayonets of 30,000 soldiers encamped permanently in a hostile country.'[18] By the end of the nineteenth century the Curragh Camp had become a divisional headquarters.

The British army was traditionally an area of potential employment for working-class Irishmen, and, while many considered Ireland a threat to British security, others considered it an abundant recruitment ground for the armed forces. The ranks comprised a wide variety of recruits, many of them coming from economically disadvantaged counties throughout Ireland. The majority of recruits came from the urban poor or agricultural working class, as joining the armed forces was seen as an opportunity to better oneself. The pay was good in comparison to what was available elsewhere and there was also an allowance paid to the spouse of the soldier while he was away on service. Others joined for adventure and to see the world. In 1830 more than half of the ordinary ranks of the British army came from Ireland and Scotland. The potato famine of 1845-51 caused a significant decrease in Irish enlistments, a problem that was exacerbated by mass emigration. However, the promise of a steady income, promotion possibilities, adventure and a pension still guaranteed a steady stream of recruits in the years that followed. A report in 1909 attested that 90 per cent of soldiers would have been hard pressed to find a job in the outside world.

---

18 Muenger, *The British Military Dilemma in Ireland 1886–1914*, p. 12.

In the late nineteenth century sweeping reforms of the armed forces were instigated by Secretary of State for War Edward Cardwell. The reforms were welcomed by many as they were a means of encouraging recruitment, improving training and linking the regular units with those of the militia. By the beginning of the twentieth century, liberal ideas, along with the increased democratisation of government and enfranchisement of a larger part of the populace, were having an effect on the composition of the armed forces. The purchase of commissions was abolished as the army developed into a more sophisticated scientific and technical organisation. Competition and promotion by merit became preferred to a system that had been based on property and patronage. Training, education and proficiency became the order of the day.[19] Reforms within the armed forces began during the Boer War in South Africa with the submission of the Army Estimates in February 1901 by the new Secretary of State for War William St John Brodrick. Reform was to continue with the formation of the Elgin Commission of 1903 and the War Office Commission of 1904, which advised ministers of the increasing demands regarding the garrisoning of its large empire, in particular India. It also warned about the need for home defence and the possibility of a war in Europe. Officer Training Colleges and reservist companies appeared in universities and local towns, and part-time military life, drilling and learning about warfare, became a popular way for many to spend their weekends.

---

19 Holmes, R., *Tommy: The British Soldier on the Western Front*, Harper Collins, London, 2005.

Government proposals stated that Britain and Ireland were to be divided into sixty-six infantry districts, twelve artillery districts and two cavalry districts. Each district would have a regimental depot, which, it was hoped, would appeal to the local patriotism of recruits. There, recruits would undergo their basic training. Building once again commenced in 1900 at the Curragh Camp as the area was enlarged to accommodate an influx of new recruits.

The training syllabus was also undergoing reform. These changes were implemented in Ireland, where army manoeuvres were held every autumn on the Curragh plains. These training exercises were the culmination of a progressive annual cycle that began during the winter months.

Booklets such as the *Field Service Regulations and Infantry Training Manual 1909* laid down the principles and details of training. Individual training consisted of physical fitness, march discipline, musketry, bayonet practice, signalling, scouting and field craft. A recruit would then progress to small unit exercises that gave way to brigade training, then divisional training and finally manoeuvres that developed into all-army manoeuvres involving thousands of soldiers. The British army paid special attention to musketry or rifle practice. At the Curragh Camp there were a number of rifle ranges that catered for different distances. The army concentrated on speeding up the rate of fire of the individual soldier. The objective was the 'mad minute', the practice of firing 15 aimed shots per minute into a 2-foot target at 300 yards.

The wide plains of the Curragh made it ideal for the deployment of cavalry and artillery. British cavalry training was considered the best in Europe and, following the Boer War, cavalry tactics had been modernised. Troopers were instructed in rifle shooting, fire discipline and the knowledge of when and where to resort to fire tactics. Military strategy had developed: modern battles were to be fought and won by infantry, covered by artillery and with the cavalry in a supportive role. Deployments consisted of engaging enemy cavalry, screening and reconnoitring for the infantry, and exploiting infantry success by pursuing the enemy and cutting their lines of retreat. While many considered this new type of warfare to have a reduced role for the cavalry, it did not deter recruits from joining the cavalry.

The army played an important role in Ireland. Those in authority believed that the army was the only force that could control Ireland, and the evidence for this could be seen in the country's bloody history.

Chapter 3

Backs Against the Wall

20 MARCH 1914, EVENING

The threat of court martial and possible execution was ever present as officers discussed the day's events. However, the loss of position and salary was considered a more urgent topic for if one refused to move northwards it could mean the end of one's career in the army.

Backed up (and advised throughout the day) by his brother John and Sir Henry Wilson, Gough refused to withdraw his resignation.

By nightfall, word was filtering back to British Headquarters on Parkgate Street in Dublin as to the decisions that were being made by British officers. On the evening of 20 March 1914, Lieutenant General Sir Arthur Paget wrote to Field Marshal Sir John French:

I must regret to have to make the following report.

The result of the interview which the GOC 5th Division and B. Gen Comg 3rd Cav Bde had with the officers in their command.

5th Div. The feeling is very bitter indeed and although the officers of the Div. as a whole are prepared to do their duty, there may be trouble with the rank and file. In any case, the attitude of the troops will not be that of willing obedience.

3rd Cav Bde including the B. Gen Commanding 58 officers are prepared to accept dismissal from the service should they be ordered to take part in active military operations against Ulster.

I have not had time to do more than interview the OC 5th Lancers in Dublin. I very much fear without good results. I shall know more tomorrow.

This Brigade could of course be usefully employed South in maintaining law and order. But if employed in this manner it would have the worst possible effect on the other arms.

I send you this information privately, which I am sure you would wish.

I am going down to the Curragh to try and put a little heart into these officers.[20]

Realising that he had to hold his command together, Major General Fergusson decided to address the various units within the 5th Division. He believed that the actions required of the army were just precautionary measures.

---

20 Imperial War Museum, 75/46/8 French Mss.

The impression left on my mind… was genuinely that the meas-
ures to be taken were primarily precautionary. The occupation of
the Government Buildings in Belfast did not seem to be in any
way intended as a provocative measure, the reason explained to us
seemed perfectly natural and reasonable. It was conceivable however
that some of the Ulster adherents might get out of hand and attack
the police, and thus initiate an outbreak, which would entail the
adoption of the preliminary measures already decided upon, and
further movement of troops in support.[21]

Fergusson feared that his own command would collapse under an avalanche of resignations and immediately decided to tour all the units in an attempt to advise them.

It was vital that the army, especially those stationed in Ireland, held together. Any sign of disaffection within the ranks may have led to a crisis that the Unionists or Nationalists could have exploited.

In Ireland troops forming the Irish Command consisted of the 5th and 6th Divisions. The 5th Division under the command of Major General Sir Charles Fergusson covered the central and north of the country and was based at the Curragh Camp in County Kildare. Having graduated from Eton and Sandhurst, Fergusson joined the Grenadier Guards in 1883. He served in the Sudan from 1896 to 1898 and became Commander of the Omdurman District in 1900. He was appointed brigadier general on the staff of the Irish Command in 1907. In 1913 he became General Officer Commanding the 5th Division

---

21 Fergusson, Sir J., *The Curragh Incident*, Faber & Faber Ltd., London, 1964, p. 78.

in Ireland and was based at the Curragh Camp in Kildare. Fergusson was considered a spit and polish commander, severe in relation to matters of discipline but respected for his competence as a commanding officer.

The 6th Division under Major General William Pulteney had its headquarters in Cork and its forces were distributed over the southern half of Ireland. A cavalry brigade was stationed with each of the two divisions, under the direct orders of the Commander-in-Chief.

Both divisions were under the overall command of the General Officer Commanding the Forces in Ireland, Lieutenant General Sir Arthur Paget. He had his administrative headquarters at Parkgate Street, Dublin, in the south-east corner of the Phoenix Park. Paget's official residence in Ireland was located in the Royal Hospital at Kilmainham, not far from Parkgate Street. It was between these two buildings that the Commander-in-Chief of British forces in Ireland would confer on a daily basis with the Officer in Charge of Administration, Major General Friend.

Both officers were career soldiers who had served at various posts throughout the British Empire. Sir Arthur Paget was commissioned into the Scots Guards in 1869 and fought during the Ashanti War in West Africa in 1873. He also served in the Sudan and in Burma before receiving an appointment as General Officer Commanding the 1st Infantry Division in 1902. In 1911 he was appointed Commander-in-Chief in Ireland. Paget was an officer who had not welcomed the changes within the army and had over the years devoted himself less to soldiering than to enjoying life. A contemporary wrote, 'the army was really much more of an occupation than a profession ... and few took any real interest in their work.'[22]

His colleague Major General Lovick Brandsby Friend had been appointed in charge of Administration at Irish Command in 1912. He had been commissioned into the Royal Engineers in 1873 and became an instructor at the Royal Military Academy at Sandhurst. He saw action at the Battle of Omdurman in the Sudan in 1898 and, like his commanding officer Paget, he was a career officer.

The battle lines over the Curragh affair had been drawn that Friday morning in Parkgate Street. The other officers stationed at the Curragh were adamant that they would not move northwards or engage the Unionists.

Since January 1911, Brigadier General Hubert Gough had been appointed to command the 3rd Cavalry Brigade at the Curragh with part of the division consisting of two regiments of cavalry, the 4th Hussars and the 16th Lancers. The remaining regiment of the Brigade, the 5th Royal Irish Lancers, were quartered at Marlborough Barracks in Dublin City.

Gough came from a distinguished military lineage: three members of his family had been awarded the coveted Victoria Cross. Having graduated from Eton College, Gough became an officer cadet at Sandhurst in 1888. A flamboyant and dashing officer, he saw service during the Boer War where he led a newly formed mounted infantry unit. He was captured and imprisoned, but he managed to escape and return to his unit. After the war he returned from South Africa a brevet colonel. From 1904 to 1906 he served as an instructor at the Staff College in

---

22 Fergusson, *The Curragh Incident*, p. 11.

Camberley before taking command of the 16th Lancers. He was described as an outstanding cavalry commander, bold in reconnaissance, dashing in action and with a genius for leadership. By 1914, at the age of forty-four, Gough was the youngest brigadier general in the army.

In 1914 Major General Gerald James Cuthbert was appointed to command the 13th Infantry Brigade, a regular brigade in the 5th Division. Having graduated from the Royal Military College, Sandhurst, Cuthbert was commissioned into the Oxfordshire Light Infantry. He saw extensive service during the Boer War, where he was mentioned in dispatches and received a brevet promotion to lieutenant colonel.

Brigadier General Stuart Peter Rolt commanded the 14th Infantry Brigade at the Curragh Camp in 1914. He had been commissioned into the York and Lancaster Regiment in 1884 and saw service in the Second Boer War before he received his appointment in Ireland.

The 5th Division field troops consisted of three infantry brigades comprising four battalions. One of these brigades, the 13th, under Brigadier General G. J. Cuthbert, was stationed in Dublin. This consisted of the 1st Battalion of the Queen's Own Royal West Kent Regiment and the 2nd Battalions of the King's Own Scottish Borderers, the Duke of Wellington's Regiment and the King's Own Yorkshire Light Infantry.

The 14th Infantry Brigade, under Brigadier General S. P. Rolt, was mostly stationed at the Curragh, but, due to the lack of barrack accommodation for its four battalions, one of them, the East Surrey regiment, spent only the summer months there, under canvas. During the winter the regiment moved to Wellington Barracks on the South Circular Road in Dublin City.

In the spring of 1914, the following regiments were stationed at the Curragh: the 2nd Battalions of the Suffolk regiment and the Manchester Regiment, and the 1st Duke of Cornwall's Light Infantry. The 5th Division Artillery was stationed nearby to the Curragh Camp, in the towns of Newbridge and Kildare. Brigadier General John Headlam, Commander, Royal Artillery, had his headquarters in Newbridge. Other units of the division, such as the Royal Engineers, the Signals, the Army Medical Corp and the Army Service Corps, were stationed at the Curragh Camp.

While most of the 5th Division was based at the Curragh, there were components in Dublin. The only parts of the division in Ulster were the three battalions of the 15th Infantry Brigade. Their commander, Brigadier General Count Gleichen, had his headquarters in Belfast with the 1st Dorsetshire Regiment, based at Victoria Barracks in the city. The Norfolk Regiment was stationed four miles from Belfast at Holywood, while the 1st Cheshire Regiment was in Londonderry. The remaining battalion, the 1st Bedfordshire Regiment, was not stationed in Ulster but was in fact stationed in the province of Leinster, at Mullingar in County Westmeath. By January 1914, the entire British army consisted of 250,000 troops, of which 30,000 troops were stationed at the Curragh, making it one of the largest training depots in Europe and, in March of 1914, one of the largest threats to stability in Ireland.

Chapter 4

A Soldier's Duty

SATURDAY, 21 MARCH

On Saturday morning, 21 March 1914, the Manchester and Suffolk Regiments were ordered to parade in the gymnasium at the Curragh Camp.

Major General Fergusson's reception was anything but cordial. He reminded the men that, although they may naturally hold private political views, officially they should not be on the side of any one political party. It was every one's duty to obey orders, to go wherever they were sent and to comply with the instructions of the political party that happened to be in power. He also reminded them that they owed loyalty to their oath to the King. Fergusson finished his address by stating that he believed that the military operation was only precautionary. The soldiers felt a sense of relief at Fergusson's clarification of the matter. He then journeyed to the other units of the division at Kildare, Newbridge and Dublin, where he gave a similar speech.

In London, the King opened his morning newspaper to discover the story of the Curragh Incident. He was outraged and immediately wrote to the Prime Minister. He stated that he 'grieved beyond words at this disastrous and irreparable catastrophe which has befallen my Army'.[23] However, the situation was about to worsen.

At the Curragh Camp that Saturday morning, Brigadier General Gough had interviewed his officers and penned the following report to Headquarters, Irish Command.

With reference to the communication from the War Office conveyed to me verbally by the Commander-in-Chief this morning, I have the honour to report the result of my interview with the officers of the brigade.

The officers are of the unanimous opinion that further information is essential before they are called upon at such short notice to take decisions so vitally affecting their whole future, and especially that a clear definition should be given of the terms 'Duty as ordered' and 'active operations' in Ulster.

If such duty consists of the maintenance of order and the preservation of property all the officers of this brigade, including myself, would be prepared to carry out that duty.

But if the duty involves the initiation of active military operations against Ulster, the following numbers of officers by regiments would respectfully, and under protest, prefer to be dismissed:

---

23 Lewis, G., Carson: *The Man Who Divided Ireland*, Hambleton, London, 2005, p. 141.

Brigade Staff, 2 officers

4th Hussars, 17 out of 19 doing duty

5th Lancers, 17 out of 20 doing duty

16th Lancers, 16 out of 16 doing duty

3rd Brigade, Royal Horse Artillery, 6 out of 13 doing duty, 'Including R.M.'

4th Field Troops, Royal Engineers, 1 out of 1 doing duty

3rd Signal Troop, Royal Engineers, 1 out of 1 doing duty

In addition, the following are domiciled in Ulster and claim protection as such:

4th Hussars, 2 officers

5th Lancers, 1 officer

3rd Brigade, Royal Horse Artillery, 2 officers[24]

Out of seventy British officers based in the Curragh Camp, fifty-seven accepted Lieutenant General Paget's offer to resign their commissions in the British army, or to accept being dismissed, rather than take up 'active operations in Ulster'.

From Kildare, Second Lieutenant R. Macleod wrote to his father:

We never knew the situation was serious until 7 o'clock on Friday night. We were then all had up in the Colonel's office and [he]

---

24 Beckett, *The Army & the Curragh Incident 1914*, p. 79.

explained the situation. I am not at liberty to say exactly what took place, but we were asked whether we should prefer to stay on and obey all orders or leave the service. Several of us, myself included, decided to leave rather than fight Ulster. We were afterwards given till today to decide. Our Divisional General and Brigadier General came to see us this morning, and said they were both in favour of Ulster, but the situation was very much graver than it seemed, for if the army split up on this question there would be a rising in India, Germany would at once declare war, and the labour situation was so serious in England that if there were no army a state of chaos would result. He said also if we went to Ulster it would not be primarily to fight Ulster but to keep order, and he hoped that the measures being taken would prevent an outbreak. The leaders of Ulster were willing to give in, but they would have difficulty in restraining their more hot-headed followers.

In view of these issues we have decided that it will be more important for us to remain in the service, however disagreeable it may be, than to look on while India and Germany does what she likes with us. We hope we have decided rightly, but it is a very difficult choice. When you have time, will you come over to Ireland some time next week, and I will be able to talk more freely, and tell you what I cannot put down on paper.[25]

Many officers were shocked at the orders and were disgusted that they had been asked to march against the Unionists; a quantity had friends and family in Ulster. The initial shock turned to anger, which resulted in a flurry of telegrams from officers in Ireland to friends, family and associates in London,

---

25 Beckett, *The Army & the Curragh Incident 1914*, p. 89.

telling them what had occurred and what choices had been forced upon them.

On receiving Gough's communiqué, Paget wired the War Office in London stating, 'Regret to report brigadier and fifty-seven officers, 3rd Cavalry Brigade, prefer to accept dismissal if ordered north.'[26]

As news of the Curragh Incident was filtering into Army Headquarters at Parkgate Street in Dublin, a series of battle plans were being prepared and another officers' meeting was convened.

If there was to be any disturbance in the north, the 5th Division supplemented by the 11th Brigade from Colchester would move to the line of the Boyne. It would be reinforced by the 1st Division from Aldershot. The 6th Division, less necessary garrisons for the South which were subsequently worked out by Generals Pulteney and Friend, would move to Dublin to be reinforced by the 18th Infantry Brigade from England. The 3 infantry Battalions from Scotland and some artillery would land in the North, and I understand would garrison certain points forming a ring around Belfast – Lisburn – Holywood – Bangor, which latter was to be a Naval base. A Naval Brigade was to be landed at Bangor.[27]

Not only was the government planning to deploy battalions of troops in Ulster, but a naval taskforce was also being made ready. The First Lord of the Admiralty Winston Churchill received a memorandum ordering naval forces to make ready:

26 Beckett, *The Army & the Curragh Incident 1914*, p. 86.
27 Fergusson, *The Curragh Incident*, p. 77.

A battle squadron will at once be placed at Lamlash, within four hours of Belfast. The question of placing a ship at Carrickfergus is to be brought before the cabinet on Tuesday or Wednesday. The Chief Secretary was given orders that the Royal Irish Constabulary should be on their guard against sudden or night attacks and that a scheme should be made for concentrating them ... in parties of 50 or more – this scheme is to be made in conjunction with the military authorities.[28]

Churchill busied himself, organising the naval task force that would carry British troops to the north if the railways refused. His naval landing parties would also be needed to secure vital coastal installations so that the army could move with ease to secure the many depots that housed arms and ammunition.

Some officers chose to ignore Paget's warning of seeking help from influential people at the War Office in Whitehall. Lieutenant Colonel I. G. Hogg sent a telegram to Winston Churchill:

Today, all officers Cavalry Brigade required to decide whether prepared to accept liability [regarding] active operations in Ulster on pain of dismissal. Enormous majority ready to accept dismissal, but later adopted proposal that authorities should be asked to define employment. Brigadier and great majority ready to undertake duties of preserving order and property provided no initiative in offensive action against Ulster contemplated. Convinced, if tactfully handled, Brigade can be saved; but if unconditional service

---

28 Asquith Papers, MS 40, Bodleian Library, Oxford.

demanded from outset, Brigadier and practically all officers will accept dismissal. Appeal to you to ensure sensible handling.[29]

However, Churchill did not reply. He may have not received the wire as he was busy planning for the deployment of his naval force.

Brigadier General S. P. Rolt wrote to Major General Sir Charles Fergusson:

With reference to the secret communication dated Parkgate, Dublin, 20 March 1914, I have interviewed all the officers in the Brigade under my command with the result that one officer has sent in an application to be permitted to disappear on the ground that his home is in Ulster, and one other officer has intimated that he cannot conscientiously carry out his duty, if ordered to proceed on operations against Ulster. All the remainder are prepared to do their duty.

I feel [it] my duty, however, as Brigade commander, to inform you of the unanimous feeling of myself, my staff, and the officers of the Brigade under my command.

We are unanimously in sympathy with the Ulster loyalists and regard with the utmost disgust the possibility of having to lead our men against them.

We are prepared to do our duty because:

We realise we must obey the orders of our King under any circumstances

---

29 Beckett, *The Army and the Curragh Incident 1914*, p. 87.

We consider it incumbent on ourselves to preserve, as far as is in our power, the British Army from disruption

I feel it is my duty to bring these points officially to your notice in order that you may know the state of the 'moral' [sic.] of the troops in the event of operations.[30]

In order to prevent further trouble in the ranks, Paget decided to address the men himself. Travelling to the Curragh Camp, he called all officers of the brigade to a meeting at 11.00 hours.

As the disgruntled officers entered the room, Paget knew he had to convince them to withdraw their resignations. He began the talk by stating that he was appalled at the officers' actions and that they were a disgrace to the army. After lambasting the men, he moved on to talk about the deployment of troops that was taking place. Precautionary movements had been carried out by troops in order to guard certain stores in Ulster and a battery of guns in Dundalk. These actions had been carried out as much out of fear of action by 'Hibernians' as by the Ulster Volunteers. British troops had been welcomed into Ulster and a large reserve camp had been established on the Boyne.

Paget took the unusual course of explaining his orders and actions to those assembled. He told them he had no intention of carrying out coercion measures against Ulster and that if he had to deploy a large body of troops into Ulster, he would ride at the head of the column himself. If he met the Ulster Volunteers he would ride forward and talk to their leadership and, if fired upon, he would not order his men to return fire. He wanted a cavalry unit to act in a reconnaissance role to prevent

---

30 Beckett, *The Army and the Curragh Incident 1914*, p. 99.

his main force from coming upon the Volunteers unexpectedly. This would prevent both sides from losing control of the situation. This suggestion only filled the officers with disdain as they contemplated the pantomime battle that would ensue. Paget reassured the men that a troop of cavalry would be deployed in the south in order to protect Protestants against possible actions by the Hibernians. His actions had been intended to prevent bloodshed, not provoke it; did his officers not trust his judgement as Commander-in-Chief? He said that he would not obey orders from politicians if he did not know they had the sanction of the King.

Paget went from puerile arguments to all-out threats as he attempted to get the officers to withdraw their resignations. He stated that all senior officers would be tried by court martial. Those assembled remained calm as they knew that they had committed no offence that would see any of them facing a military court.

Paget left his audience with nothing but a bad impression. What surprised many of those who listened to Paget's address was that he never appealed to their honour or sense of duty but continually talked about the ruin of their careers. Even after Paget's address, the situation was far from under control. The Secretary of State for War J. E. B. Seely gave Paget permission to suspend any officer tendering his resignation.

In his diary Sir Henry Wilson declared himself 'more than ever determined to resign, but I cannot think of a really good way of doing it'.

In London, Paget's telegram and news of events in Ireland caused consternation among politicians and army alike. On hearing of Churchill's preparations to dispatch the 3rd Battle

Fleet to Lamlash, Prime Minister Asquith countermanded the order and directed it to be stood down. Any orders to prepare an attack or show force in Ulster were immediately cancelled.

With the situation worsening, General Gough and Colonels Parker, 5th Lancers, MacEwan, 16th Lancers and Colonel Hogg of the 4th Hussars were ordered to go to London immediately. They left that night.

Chapter 5

Standoff

SATURDAY, 21 MARCH 1914, EVENING

After the day's events, Lieutenant General Sir Arthur Paget sent a telegram to the Secretary of State for War J. E. B. Seely:

> *General Fergusson assured me late tonight that but for the attitude of Col. Parker & rest of Brigade would have withdrawn resignations.*[31]

While many of the officers and men of the 5th Division decided to remain at their posts, Brigadier General Gough and his officers in the 3rd Cavalry Brigade were adamant that they were in no way going to war against Ulster.

Events were moving rapidly and Paget knew that he had to stop the spread of any dissention within the ranks of the army, a task easier said than done.

---

31 Beckett, *The Army and the Curragh Incident 1914*, p. 28.

In a letter to a friend, Gough later confided:

But when I come back to look at it all, I have to be honest and admit that truly Ulster was not the first thing on my mind when I came out of the conference with Sir Arthur Paget. What made me furious was that the War Office authorities had conceived and Arthur Paget accepted that they could bully officers by giving them a choice of doing something or being dismissed. What a way to run things.[32]

Many of the officers knew that they had a lot to lose if they resigned. Being an officer could be a very expensive career. An officer had to provide his own uniforms, furniture, travel kit and servant's uniform. An officer in an infantry regiment, such as the Guards, could be expected to pay an estimated £400 a year, while a cavalry officer had even more expenses as he needed a variety of horse types, such as a charger, two hunters and three polo ponies. All officers had to pay mess contributions and sports clubs membership, and to contribute to the many social events that took place throughout the year. In order to cover all these expenses, officers had to have a private income as the army pay was insufficient. Families often provided an income for an officer, and those who left the army in dishonour often found themselves unemployable and destitute as their families refused to finance them.

Young officers were trained by efficient non-commissioned officers or NCOs, the senior officers responsible for company accounts, kit inspections and other camp routines. However, if

32 Farrar-Hockley, A., *Goughie: A Biography of General Sir Hubert de la Poer Gough*, London, Hart-Davis, MacGibbon, 1975, PIII, p. 83.

one was the orderly officer for the day, it meant a day full of perfunctory duties, such as turning out the guard, checking on prisoners in the guardroom, and inspecting the cookhouse, the canteens and everything else in the camp.

The troops of the Irish Command consisted of two infantry divisions with their artillery and auxiliary units and two cavalry brigades. The life for ordinary ranks and junior officers was one of routine. While initial training took up most of a recruit's time, it was ceremonial duties that required considerable preparation, as Trooper Robert Lloyd recalled:

After breakfast the saddle and all its appendages were brown polished; head-kit [bridle] blackened; brow band and girth pipe clayed; bit and stirrups burnished; brass head-stall and breastplate polished, and all buckles polished inside and out. The horse was then saddled, and sheep-skin and cloak placed in position. He was then tied short, and somebody asked to keep an eye on him lest he lie down. There followed a dash upstairs to shave, wash and dress.... For the King's Guard there were actually two parades. The first was on foot. We were marched onto the parade ground by squadrons. The inspection which ensued was something of an ordeal. The Adjutant, Quartermaster and RCM turned everything inside out.[33]

Before ceremonial duties, the second inspection was carried out by the riding master.

The mounted inspection was a thousand times worse than on foot.... We sat there like so many graven images. When your turn

---

33 Spunner, B. H., *Horse Guards*, Macmillan, London, 2006, p. 443.

came one would examine your horse's mane; another would pick up a hoof to see if it had been washed out; a third would beat a tattoo with his whip on your sheep-skin in the hope of making the dust fly. Perched up in the air as you now were, any of them could look at the insides of your boots and spurs. Unless you had a kicking horse there was not the flimsiest chance of getting away with anything.[34]

The officers' mess was the centre of social life within the camp and it influenced all aspects of an officer's life. For unmarried officers, the mess served three main purposes: a cabin for residence, a place for wining and dining, and a space for entertaining relatives and friends. For married officers, the mess provided a social space where they could gather for moments of relaxation and conversation with their fellow officers. Mess etiquette and customs were strictly adhered to and any officers in breach of the rules and regulations were subjected to severe penalties such as disciplinary action or fines.

The local gentry organised social occasions where officers were invited to take part. Parties, hunts and balls were plentiful, and officers in their dress uniforms were familiar sights at social gatherings. It was at such events that soldiers discussed politics and the state of the country. Topics included nationalism, unionism, the suffragette movement and the rise of socialism.

Brigadier General Hubert Gough wrote:

During the first three years of my command of the 3rd Cavalry Brigade life was pleasant but uneventful. As usual in Ireland,

---

34 Spunner, *Horse Guards*, p. 446.

hunting, races and horse shows were our chief amusement when we were not soldiering, as they were of the people among whom we lived. None of us cavalry soldiers were much interested in Irish politics, and as far as we were aware, the people apart from the professional politicians, were not much more interested either.[35]

While many soldiers distanced themselves from such conversations or kept their opinions to themselves, there were others who openly supported a variety of causes. In Ireland, the cause that gathered most support among the upper ranks in the army was that of unionism, and the question often discussed was that of Home Rule for Ireland. However, that question would soon require an answer.

---

35 Gough, *Soldiering On*, p. 98.

Chapter 6

Blood Oath

The crisis at the Curragh Camp had been precipitated by events in Ulster two years earlier.

On 28 September 1912, on what became known as Ulster Day, 471,414 unionists signed the Solemn League and Covenant, a document of protest against the introduction of Home Rule in Ireland:

> *Being convinced in our consciences that Home Rule would be disastrous to the material well-being of Ulster as well as the whole of Ireland, subversive of our civil and religious freedom, destructive of our citizenship and perilous to the unity of the Empire, we, whose names are under-written, men of Ulster, loyal subjects of His Gracious Majesty King George V, humbly relying on the God whom our fathers in days of stress and trial confidently trusted, do hereby pledge ourselves in solemn Covenant throughout this our time of threatened calamity to stand by one another in defending for ourselves and our children our cherished possession of equal citizenship in the United Kingdom and in using all means which*

may be found necessary to defeat the present conspiracy to set up a Home Rule Parliament in Ireland. And in the event of such a Parliament being forced upon us we further solemnly and mutually pledge ourselves to refuse to recognise its authority. In sure confidence that God will defend the right we hereto subscribe our names.

And further, we individually declare that we have not already signed this Covenant.

The Ulster Covenant was based on the old Scottish Covenant of 1580. Though the paper permitted the signatories to profess loyalty to the King of England, it also warned the government that the men of Ulster would use any and all means possible to prevent a conspiracy that would see Home Rule established in Ireland. James Craig organised the event with Edward Carson, Lord Charles Beresford, Lord Londonderry and J. H. Campbell among the first signatories to the document. Ulster Day was an attempt by Ulster Unionists to convince the British electorate of their determination to fight any attempt to implement Home Rule in Ireland. An equivalent number of people signed copies of the Covenant at rallies in other parts of the country. The Covenant was a huge success as it saw the emergence of a mass movement of defiance.

However, in the months that followed, Unionist demonstrations and protests made little impact on the Irish policy of British ministers. The Home Rule Bill continued to make slow but steady progress through Westminster. Unionist supporters urged for more drastic and radical action. A provisional government was established and plans were set in place to evacuate women and children if civil war erupted.

Defiance of the possible implementation of Home Rule was epitomised in a popular rhyme of the time:

Sir Edward Carson had a cat

It sat upon the fender

And every time it saw a mouse

It shouted 'No Surrender!'

In January 1913, the Ulster Unionist Council began to drill a force of men that were to become known as the Ulster Volunteer Force (UVF). It was intended to build up an army of 100,000 men with supporting corps such as a medical corps, motorised units, a nursing corps and an intelligence corps. The UVF was seen as a means of preserving party unity and discipline as well as a possible means of exerting pressure on the British government. It was also there to resist by force, if necessary, an all-Ireland government based in Dublin.

Sir George Richardson, a retired English general of the Indian army, and Colonel Hacket Pain, who was appointed as his Chief of Staff, commanded the force. One of the chief advisers of this new force was Lord Roberts, a veteran of the Boer War. Alarmingly, several serving British army officers such as Sir Henry Wilson also supported the UVF. Wilson, like many others, came from a family of Irish Protestant landlords who feared that Home Rule or partition of any kind would threaten or destroy their way of life.

In 1893, Lord Wolseley, while holding the post of Commander-in-Chief in Ireland, warned of the possibility of the army working in collusion with Unionists:

If ever our troops are brought into collision with the loyalists of Ulster and blood is shed, it will shake the whole foundations upon which our army rests so much that I feel our army will never be the same again. Many officers will resign to join Ulster and there will be such a host of retired officers in the Ulster ranks that men who would stand by the government, no matter what it did, will be worse than half-hearted in all they do. No army could stand such a strain upon it.[36]

Thousands of young men rallied to the UVF flag in support of Ulster. By the end of 1913 the UVF had 90,000 members and a full complement of ex-British army officers stationed at their headquarters in Belfast's Old Town Hall. The force was organised on a county basis, and divided into regiments, battalions and sections depending on the strengths of each of the northern counties. Local estate owners allowed their lands to be used as weekend training camps. The companies drilled using dummy wooden rifles. The national newspapers ridiculed the Unionist force in relation to their lack of weapons. Broadsheets such as the *Freeman's Journal* alluded in its columns to the 'Orange Farce' and 'Playing at Rebellion'. However, the situation was rapidly escalating.

The British officer commanding the 15th Infantry Brigade in Ulster, Brigadier General Count Gleichen, recalled his evening walks in the countryside just outside Belfast:

During the summer, if one went for an after-dinner walk, as I have often done, one would hear voices and words of command; and

---

36 Wolseley to the Duke of Cambridge, 23 April 1893, from Verner, Col. Willoughby, *The Military Life of H. R. H. the Duke of Cambridge*, vol. 2, London, John Murray, 1905, p. 381.

looking over the hedge, one would see small bodies of men drilling in the fields in the dark. On most of these properties men who did not join the force were looked at askance and given the cold shoulder. [87]

Financial aid came from a number of sources, including those serving within the British army. A letter sent from Gough Barracks at Secunderabad in India to the editor of the *Belfast Weekly News* by W. McDowell, R. Shields and 'Ulsterman in India' reveals the extent of the support for the organisation:

By request of the Loyal Ulstermen of the 1st Battalion, Royal Inniskilling Fusiliers we have commenced a collection in aid of the 'Ulster Defence Fund' and send as our first donation the sum of £18.6s.8d.

Though serving beyond the seas, we follow with the keenest interest the volunteer movement in Ulster, and time-expired men going home this trooping season are looking forward to taking their place in the ranks with their fellow countrymen. 'The Flag must be kept flying', and the motto of 'No Surrender' upheld. Those who will still be serving their King in India, and cannot go home for some years, sincerely hope that Ulster will win, and nothing will shake their loyalty to the Union. We are sorry we could not send a larger donation, but we hope to do better next time. [38]

With the signing of the Solemn League and Covenant and the rise in paramilitary groups, Prime Minister Asquith was coming under

---

37 Beckett, *The Army & the Curragh Incident 1914*, p. 4.
38 Beckett, *The Army & the Curragh Incident 1914*, p. 51.

increasing pressure from the King to reach a solution. On 11 August 1913, King George V sent a memorandum to the Prime Minister expressing his growing anxiety in relation to the looming crisis in Ulster. He suggested that an all-party conference be called to explore the possibility of a settlement. Asquith knew the King was under pressure from a number of senior Conservatives and replied that the King should not become involved in the Home Rule crisis. Asquith stated that, when Home Rule was finally implemented, Ulster would experience a state of turmoil and possible riot, but that talk of a civil war was alarmist.

However, the corridors of the War Office in London echoed with concerns. On 25 September 1913, Field Marshal Sir John French wrote a report to Lord Stamfordham, Private Secretary to King George V, outlining the army's stance in relation to the developing situation in the North of Ireland:

- *I have received verbal commands from the King to place before His Majesty in writing through you, and without reference to any other person whatsoever, my personal views as to the effect which would be produced in the Army if the Troops were called upon to oppose an Armed Resistance by Ulster to Home Rule. I was asked by His Majesty to observe the utmost secrecy in carrying out these instructions and this command has been strictly complied with.*

- *I believe the spirit of discipline which permeates throughout all ranks of His Majesty's Troops to be of the highest order. They would as a body obey unflinchingly and without question the absolute commands of the King no [matter] what their private opinions might be. If the spirit did not form the foundation of the whole military structure the army would be unreliable and unfit for the purpose for which it exists.*

- *Men however are only mortal and I have no hesitation in saying that discipline of His Majesty's Troops would be subjected to a great strain if they were called upon to fire on men who are not only their Compatriots but are flying their own flag which is indeed the emblem of their aspiration. Whether in flying that flag and taking up this attitude the Ulster men would have public right and reason on their side is a matter of opinion, but the arguments in favour of such a view must infallibly impress themselves on the minds of a large proportion of any given body of thinking people.*

- *Whilst then I think that the precept enunciated in the 2nd paragraph of this letter is absolutely vital to the existence of an efficient army, I feel … there are many good officers and men, not possessing any logical minds, who would be led to think they were best serving their King and country either by refusing to march against the Ulster men or openly joining their ranks.*

- *From this consideration I draw the conclusion that whilst the Army as a whole would obey, without hesitation, the orders of the King, its discipline would be subjected to a severe trial and there would be larger or smaller defections from its ranks, both of officers and men.*

- *It is because I have strongly felt these apprehensions that I have from the first advocated dealing with such cases of defections as have hitherto arisen in a drastic manner in order to impress upon all serving officers the necessity for [sic.] abstaining from any political controversy.*[39]

In November 1913, respected academic Eoin McNeill suggested that Irish Nationalists should seize the opportunity and form

---

39 R.A. GV K. 2553(2) 35; IWM, 75/46/8. French Mss

a paramilitary organisation to bolster nationalist demands for self-government. The leaders of the Irish Republican Brotherhood seized the opportunity and assisted in the launch of a new nationalist organisation known as the Irish Volunteers. This was the second parliamentary organisation to emerge that November: the Irish Citizen Army under James Connolly also took to the streets.

At a speech in Dublin City, Andrew Bonar Law, the Conservative leader, urged the army in Ireland not to fight against Ulster. The civil war which threatened the country would not be possible if the army refused to fight.[40]

Meanwhile, meetings between the various organisations continued throughout the autumn and winter months of 1913. Speaking in the House of Commons, Prime Minister Asquith said:

What is Ulster? I have a very useful map in which Ulster is coloured. By looking at that map, I see that, dividing Ulster according to its representation – leaving population for the moment – between those who are in favour and those who are against Home Rule, the whole of the North-West, the whole of the South, the larger part of the middle – by the middle I mean the County of Tyrone – are almost unanimously in favour of Home Rule. That is a geographical fact; there can be no dispute about it whatever. Under this Amendment the whole of Donegal, which returns a united Nationalist representation, the whole of Tyrone, of which three divisions as compared with one return a representation in favour of Home Rule, the whole of Monaghan and Cavan, part

40 *The Times*, 29 November 1913.

*of Fermanagh, part of Armagh, although they have a preponder-
atingly [sic] Nationalist population and are represented in this
House by Members in favour of Home Rule, would be excluded
from the benefit of the Home Rule Bill. That cannot be disputed.
It is not disputed by the right Hon. Gentleman. In point of fact,
as was clearly indicated in Committee, there are only two counties in Ulster which return a uniform Unionist representation
– Londonderry and Antrim.*

*If you look at the population, how does the matter stand? In what
I will call, for convenience and brevity, Unionist Ulster – that is,
the part represented [in] this House by Unionist Members – the
population is, roughly speaking, 690,000 Protestants, 270,000
Roman Catholics. On the other hand, if you look at Home Rule
Ulster, that part which is represented here by Nationalists or
Members in favour of Home Rule, the Roman Catholics, there
are 436,000, and Protestants 194,000. If you take the province
of Ulster as a whole, roughly speaking – I do not pretend to precise
mathematical accuracy – there are in it nine Protestants to seven
Catholics. Anxious and most anxious as he may be to conciliate
all reasonable opposition, and above all, to give such effect as he
can to whatever is reasonable, to whatever can be given effect to in
apprehensions and susceptibilities of Protestant Ulster – how is it
possible, in the face of figures such as these, for anyone who accepts
the principle of this Bill, to justify the exclusion of the whole province of Ulster from the operation of the Bill.... It is indeed, as I
have said, a claim which I do not think you will find the people of
Great Britain will ever recognise.*[41]

41 Asquith, H. H., Report Stage of the Third Home Rule Bill.

In December 1913 the government imposed a ban on the importation of arms and ammunition into Ireland. However, this would not deter the Unionists; in January 1914, Belfast businessman Major Frederick Crawford travelled to Germany with the intention of purchasing arms and ammunition.

As events were unfolding in Ireland, British Military Intelligence was growing increasingly concerned about the possible threat of a civil war. If a threat was forthcoming, a plan of action would be needed, a plan that would secure Ireland and England against those who would attempt to over-throw the government and the King.

Alarmists within the War Office in London were becoming concerned about possible raids on military depots in Ireland.

Brigadier General Count Gleichen, as mentioned, knew of the drilling being carried out by the UVF as he had encountered them during his after-dinner strolls along the country roads in the evening. His own personal view of the situation in Ulster was that Unionist leaders were resolved to take no provocative action and to repress any disorder.

However, it was Gleichen's district of command that concerned those in the War Office the most. There were several places within the north-east of the country where army depots held a considerable amount of rifles and ammunition that could be seized by the Ulstermen and used to equip a small army.

Carrickfergus Castle on the north-western shore of Belfast Lough held 85 tonnes of ordnance. Victoria Barracks in Belfast City, where the Dorsetshire Regiment was stationed, held an estimated 30 tonnes of ammunition and rifles. In Omagh in County Tyrone, Armagh town and Enniskillen in

County Fermanagh there were another 30 tonnes of ammunition. At Dundalk, the Royal Field Artillery had three batteries of eighteen guns and a complement of ammunition for the weapons.

Much of the information that was being received by the War Office was unverified as Ireland lacked any military intelligence network. The British Cabinet depended on reports that were submitted by the police in Ireland but these were lacking in any solid information. Police reports stated that the UVF numbered 80,000 men with 17,000 weapons and that if the Home Rule Bill reached the statute books the UVF would proclaim a provisional government. *The Irish Times* newspaper reported on the large number of resignations from the Royal Irish Constabulary, whose members were concerned that they might be used against any unionist force since the constabulary in Ireland was a paramilitary force that would be called out before the regular army in a crisis.

The men state that when they undertook what almost amounted to military duty in the past a different condition of affairs prevailed and they were not smarting under grievances such as those from which they suffered at present. It is generally anticipated by them that should a serious outbreak of disorder occur in the North and if the Ulster Volunteer Force, armed and trained men, be mobilised, the first thing which Dublin Castle will do will be to collect an immense force of Constabulary in the disturbed area for what will be military duty pure and simple. It will result in wholesale resignations from the Force in every province in Ireland, and particularly in Ulster. The conditions of service for the rank and file at present are so deplorable that all who can do so, without serious monetary loss, will at once comply with the rule on leaving the service and give one month's notice.[42]

The number of alarming reports emanating from Ireland prompted the British Cabinet to appoint a special committee to deal with Ulster. It consisted of Chief Secretary Augustine Birrell, Attorney General Sir John Simon, Secretary of State for War J. E. B. Seely and First Lord of the Admiralty Winston Churchill, with the Marquis of Crewe as chairman. Crewe was chosen because he had been Lord Lieutenant of Ireland from 1892–95.

In December 1913, Seely, worrying about the army and its behaviour, issued a cabinet memorandum that read:

The law clearly lays down that a soldier is entitled to obey an order to shoot only if that order is reasonable under the circumstances. No one, from General Officer to Private, is entitled to use more force than is required to maintain order and the safety of life and property. No soldier can shelter himself behind an order given by a superior, if in fact that order is unreasonable and outrageous.

If, therefore, officers and men in the army were led to believe that they might be called upon to take some outrageous action, for instance, to massacre a demonstration of Orangemen, who were causing no danger to the lives of their neighbours, bad as were the effects on discipline in the Army, nevertheless it was true that they were in fact and in law justified in contemplating refusal to obey.

---

42 *Irish Times*, 30 February 1914, p. 4.

There never had been and was not now any intention of giving outrageous and illegal orders to the Troops to crush helpless Ulstermen. The law must be respected and obeyed.

What had to be faced was the possibility of action being required ... where the police were unable to hold their own .... There had been attempts ... to dissuade troops from obeying lawful orders given to them when supporting the civil power. This amounted to a suggestion that officers or men could pick and choose between lawful and reasonable orders, saying that in one case they would obey and not in another .... Such a state of affairs would of course be impossible. The Army had been quite steady. During the past year, there had not been brought to the notice of the authorities one single case of lack of discipline in this respect.

... I plan to inform the Commanders-in-Chief ... that I would hold each of them individually responsible to see there was no conduct in their commands subversive to discipline. They would let it be clearly understood that any such conduct will be dealt with forthwith under the King's Regulations. If any officer should tender his resignation they would ask for his reasons, and if he indicated in his reply that he desired to choose which order he would obey I would at once submit to the King that the officer would be cashiered.[43]

Though the corridors of the War Office echoed with rumour and innuendo, the memorandum issued by Seely reveals that there was a serious worry within the army and the government that there could very well be a problem with possible disobedience among army officers. Two days after Seely's memorandum

---

43 CAB 17/117/87 British Public Records Office J. E. B. Seely 9/12/13.

was issued, British authorities seized a shipment of arms destined for the UVF in Ulster. The authorities secured the weapons in the Belfast Custom House but were worried that the UVF might attempt to take back the weapons by force. This added to the rising concerns of the government in London.

Chief Secretary Augustine Birrell issued a memo in relation to the Ulster situation in early March 1914. In the paper he attempted to play down the state of affairs, claiming that, though the UVF were still drilling, their leadership did not really think that the situation would spiral out of control and into civil war.

In early March 1914, Prime Minister Asquith attempted to appease both Unionists and Nationalists by suggesting the exclusion of four counties from Home Rule. Counties Down, Londonderry, Fermanagh and Antrim could be, he suggested, excluded for a period of six years. John Redmond reluctantly accepted this proposal but Carson refused it, stating that it was 'a sentence of death with a stay of execution for six years'.[44] This was to be the first proposal of partition for Ireland. Many of those in political circles believed that once Home Rule had been granted the Unionists would reluctantly accept it and in time cooperate with a nationalist government. However, the determination of Unionist opposition was seriously underestimated. Many politicians still believed that the Ulster Unionists were playing a game of bluff.

On Saturday, 14 March, Churchill delivered an inflammatory speech in Bradford that caused consternation throughout the country:

---

44 Lewis, *Carson: The Man Who Divided Ireland*, p. 105.

If Ulstermen extend the hand of friendship, it will be clasped by Liberals and by their nationalist countrymen in all good faith and in all good will; but if there is no wish for peace; if every concession that is made is spurned and exploited; if every effort to meet their views is only to be used as a means of breaking down Home Rule and of barring the way to the rest of Ireland; if Ulster is to become a tool in party calculations; if the civil and Parliamentary systems under which we have dwelt so long, and our fathers before us, are to be brought to the rude challenge of force; if the government and the Parliament of this great country and great Empire are to be exposed to menace and brutality; if all the loose, wanton and reckless chatter we have been forced to listen to these many months is in the end to disclose a sinister and revolutionary purpose, then I can only say to you, 'Let us go forward together and put these grave matters to the proof.'[45]

Churchill was quoted in the press as saying 'that there were worse things than bloodshed on an extended scale'. He described the Ulster provisional government as 'a self-elected body, composed of persons who, to put it plainly, are engaged in a treasonable conspiracy', hinting at 'a sinister and revolutionary purpose' behind it. He said, 'Let us go forward together and put these grave matters to the proof.' While Churchill's speech contained a substantial element of imprecision, these last words outraged Unionist politicians who claimed that it was deliberately provocative and foreshadowed a high-handed action against the 'loyalists' of Ulster.[46]

---

45 Langworth, *Churchill in His Own Words*, p. 223.

46 Fergusson, *The Curragh Incident*.

Churchill's speech, together with his orders for the British navy 3rd Battle Squadron's forthcoming practice that was to take place off the Isle of Arran, only an hour's sailing from the Northern Irish coast, contributed to the idea that a plan to coerce Ulster to come under a Dublin parliament was underway.

On the same day that Churchill spoke in Bradford, the following orders were issued from the War Office by Lieutenant General Paget. They were signed by the Secretary of the Army Council.

Sir,

I am commanded by the Army Council to inform you that in Consequence of reports which have been received by His Majesty's Government that attempts may be made in various parts of Ireland by evil-disposed persons to obtain possession of arms, ammunition, and other Government stores, it is considered advisable that you should at once take special precautions for safeguarding depots and other places where arms or stores are kept, as you may think advisable.

It appears from the information received that Armagh, Omagh, Carrickfergus, and Enniskillen are insufficiently guarded, being especially liable to attack. You will, therefore, please to take the necessary steps and report to this office.

Officers in command of all barracks where guns, small arms, ammunition, and other government stores are located should be warned that they will be held responsible that all measures to ensure the safety of the stores, & c., under their custody are taken, and that at no time should barracks or buildings be left without adequate armed guards.

I am to add that although certain places have been specifically referred to above, the intention is that no steps should be omitted to ensure the safety of Government arms and stores in the south as well as in the north of Ireland.

I am, & c.,

B.R. Cubitt.[47]

Churchill's actions prompted Edward Carson to verbally attack the First Lord of the Admiralty in the House of Commons. Carson immediately left the building and caught the Belfast mail train, leaving those behind pondering if he had gone to Ulster to proclaim an insurgent provisional government in the province.

---

47 White Paper, part I, no. 2.

Chapter 7

Enigma

16–19 MARCH 1914

A number of days previously, on Monday, 16 March, Secretary of State for War J. E. B. Seely wired Lieutenant General Paget asking him what steps had been taken regarding the security of the military depots in the north of Ireland. Paget replied the following day, stating that he was satisfied with the strength of the garrison at Enniskillen. He was in the process of increasing the garrison at Carrickfergus and was taking steps to remove the arms and ammunition from Armagh and Omagh to a more secure location. However, Paget was reluctant to move troops into the province in case the action exacerbated the situation.

A letter written by J. E. B. Seely and despatched from the War Office to Field Marshal Sir John French added a new dimension to the threatening crisis:

You have put to me the question of how best to meet the situation which would arise if simultaneously with serious disturbances in

Ireland a menace from Germany were to arise. I think you may safely proceed on the following assumptions.

- *At the present time there is a possibility that the Ulster Volunteer Force, numbering some 100,000 men might take aggressive action which the Executive would have to meet. This would require a large mobile force of the Regular Army, with transport and artillery on an adequate scale.*
- *Apart from this possibility, the actual position is that the Army is required in support of the civil power, i.e. to safeguard Government property, to maintain law and order, and to protect the police and other Govt. Servants in the execution of their duty. This situation does not require a large mobile force with transport and artillery.*
- *There is a possibility that Germany may take advantage of the present disturbances to attack, or threaten to attack us.*

The question is, can (i) and (iii) coincide. In my considered judgement they cannot, and for the following reason.

Any serious menace of hostile attack from outside would have the result (a) that the Govt. and the Opposition would agree to postpone a settlement of their difference until the outside menace had been dealt with, (b) the Ulster Force would cease aggressive action.

This is my individual opinion, and no other is obtainable; but it is based on an intimate knowledge of the leaders of the three parties.

If my view is accurate, the urgent problem is to find a solution for (ii) combined with (iii) together with civil disturbances on a large scale in this country.

Will you work this problem, or series of problems out.

I should add that for practical purposes of administration so long as the present situation continues or not more than three battalions of infantry are sent from Great Britain, the matter can properly be regarded as an action in support of the civil power not seriously jeopardizing our international position and thus properly dealt with through the ordinary channels. Should further reinforcements beyond the three battalions be required, the matter would become one of the General Staff under your special direction and you will act accordingly.[48]

Paget was ordered to report to the War Office in London on 18 March to attend a series of emergency meetings. Those also in attendance were prominent cabinet members as well as the Chief of the Imperial General Staff Field Marshal Sir JohnFrench, Adjutant General Sir Spencer Ewart and Major General Sir Nevil Macready. Prime Minister Asquith and the special committee mentioned earlier were also present. The diary of Sir Spencer Ewart reveals what was discussed at the meeting:

We had a conference at the War Office at 12 noon re Ulster crisis.

There were present Colonel Seely, Sir John French, myself, Sir Nevil Macready, Earl of Crewe, Mr. Winston Churchill, Prince Louis of Battenburg, Mr. Birrell, Sir A. Paget, and Mr. G Nicolson, Seely's Private Secretary.

We decided on certain measures and movement of troops designed for protection of barracks and depots where arms and ammunition

---

48 IWM, 75/46/8 French Mss.

and mobilisation stores are collected. The conference was resumed at 6 p.m. in the Prime Minister's house, 10 Downing Street, where there were present: The Prime Minister, Colonel Seely, Mr. Lloyd George, Mr. Birrell, Sir A. Paget, Sir John French, self, Sir N. Macready, Mr. Winston Churchill.

The whole question was discussed; it was decided, inter alia, that Sir Nevil Macready was to proceed to Belfast to become, at the opportune moment, Military Governor of Belfast. Birrell under-took to put Commissioner Smith and the R.I.C. Belfast under him. One of the Battle Squadrons was on its way, in any case, from Arosa Bay to Lamlash and could pick up any troops at Kingstown and take them north. This seemed to be a quite sensible suggestion.[49]

Troop deployments continued to be discussed at meetings the following day and, though no written records were taken at many of the meetings, instructions transmitted by Paget to his headquarters in Dublin reveal the lengths to which the British government were willing to go in order to secure Ulster:

- *A Battalion of the 14th Infantry Brigade would be moved to Newry and Dundalk.*
- *Carrickfergus would be reinforced by troops from Dublin.*
- *Enniskillen, Omagh and Armagh would be reinforced by troops from Mullingar.*

---

49 Diary of John Spencer Ewart, 18 March 1914, Williamwood Papers, National Register of Archives, Scotland.

- *The Dorsets Battalion, located in Belfast, would be moved to Holywood in case an attempt was made to blockade them within the city.*
- *General Macready would go to Belfast to take over as military governor when he considered it necessary.[50]*

Despite these orders being relayed in secret, the leader of the opposition in Parliament Andrew Bonar Law and Ulster Unionist Sir Edward Carson were kept fully informed of the operation at the War Office by the Director of Military Operations Major General Sir Henry Wilson. Born in Ballinalee, County Longford, Wilson had entered the army through the 'Militia back door'. This meant that officers holding a commission in the militia or yeomanry could bypass the Royal Military Academy at Sandhurst altogether by taking a competitive examination for a direct commission. A garrulous and ambitious Irishman, he entered the Rifle Brigade and during the Third Burmese War in 1885, he received a facial wound that earned him the title 'the ugliest man in the British army'. A protégé of Lord Roberts, Wilson had risen through the ranks and by 1914 held the rank of major general. He was a staunch loyalist and was considered by many to be an inveterate intriguer who enjoyed inciting adversity between the military and Parliament. His support of the Ulster Unionists is revealed in his diary entries:

9th November 1913: I went to see Bonar Law at ¼ to 10 this morning and spent 1½ hours with him. He was quite charming to me. I told him there was much talk in the army, and that if we

---

50 Beckett, *The Army and the Curragh Incident 1914*, p. 60.

*were ordered to coerce Ulster there would be wholesale defection. He
fully realised this and told me Stamfordham had been to see him
yesterday and had said that in his opinion 40 pc. of officers and men
would leave the army. Personally I put the pc. much lower, but very
serious. I then told them of Cecil's idea that Carson should pledge
the Ulster troops to fight for England if she was at war. I pointed
out that a move like this would render the imployment [sic.] of force
against Ulster more impossible than ever. He was much pleased with
the suggestion and at once tried to get Carson on the telephone. He
was, however, away for the day. Bonar Law will see him tomorrow.*[51]

Wilson often engaged Field Marshal Sir John French in conversation, gleaning bits of information in relation to the meetings that were ongoing behind closed doors. He then used this to his own advantage by passing it on to the Conservatives or the Unionists. His dislike for the Liberal government fuelled his efforts in discrediting the government and influencing junior officers on political opinions. On hearing of the planned deployment of troops in Ulster, Wilson wrote in his diary that:

*[T]hey are contemplating scattering troops all over Ulster as though
it was a Pontypool coal strike. Sir John pointed out that this was
opposed to all true strategy etc., but was told that the political situation necessitates this dispersion. He said that, as far as he could
see, the government were determined to see this thing through. He
did not say where the troops were to be sent.... [L]ater I dined with
Charlie Hunter, where were Milner, Doctor 'Jim', and Carson. A
long and most interesting talk.*[52]

51 Callwell, *Field Marshall Sir Henry Wilson*, His Life and Diaries, vol. 1, p. 128.
52 Callwell, *Field Marshall Sir Henry Wilson, His Life and Diaries*, vol. 1, p. 139.

The conference continued the following day, 19 March, without Asquith, who had a meeting with the King. The King saw the Prime Minister and discussed the developments of the political situation including Churchill's speech at Bradford on 14 March.

At the meeting in the cabinet rooms, Paget raised a number of concerns in relation to the deployment of British troops in Ulster. He reiterated the fact that any movement of troops in Ulster would create a situation of active resistance from loyalists in the province. However, this concern was dismissed and he was reminded that, as Commander-in-Chief, he had full discretionary powers to deploy his forces as he saw fit. He also raised the question of the logistics involved of moving troops to Ulster, especially if the Great Northern Railway refused to move them. Churchill promised support from the royal navy. Paget's final concern related to the possible behaviour of his officers if they were ordered to move north. Seely stated that officers ordered to act in support of the civil power should not be permitted to resign their commissions but must, if they refused to obey orders, be dismissed from the army. Officers that resided in Ulster were permitted to request a transfer.

During the day, Paget sent orders to his second in command Major General L. B. Friend, ordering that troops at the Curragh Camp were to be issued with ten rounds of ammunition and five extra rounds per man were to be issued to each corporal in charge of a barrack room. All over the camp the number of guards was doubled and special picquets were established at a set distance outside the camp. Troops began to mobilise and Brigadier General Gleichen, the officer commanding forces in the province of Ulster, was ordered to move his men to more strategic positions.

Paget returned to Ireland on the evening of 19 March and immediately wired instructions to his unit commanders, Generals Fergusson, Rolt, Cuthbert and Gough, to meet him on Friday at Army Headquarters in Parkgate Street. Paget was in a state of excitement.

In relation to all the meetings in London, Paget received no written orders from the War Office, a factor that was to have insurmountable repercussions.

As the officers read Paget's telegram, they realised that a situation was unfolding and that they would be required to 'make ready'. The events that were to unfold would threaten the security and the stability of the country.

Chapter 8

On The Carpet

SUNDAY, 22 MARCH

After a brief breakfast, Brigadier General Hubert Gough, accompanied by his brother John, set off at a brisk walk towards the War Office in Whitehall, London. They began their short journey with a good deal of trepidation. Travelling from Aldershot, John Gough informed his brother that the War Office intended to take the line that there had been a complete misunderstanding and the alternatives put forward by Paget should never had been mentioned and that all the officers were to be reinstated. There were to be no court martials or repercussions by the military for any officer who had tendered his resignation. However, Hubert Gough was incensed and was very suspicious of his superiors, both civil and military. He had made up his mind that the best option open to him was to resign from the service.

A few minutes before 10.00 hours Hubert and John Gough entered the War Office. Leaving their caps and swagger sticks at reception, they made their way into an anteroom where they met Colonel Parker of the 5th Lancers and Colonel Ewan of the 16th Lancers, who had also been summoned to attend the meeting. They sat side by side on a fixed wooden seat which ran the length of the room with their backs against the wall. These seats commanded a view of the door, and from this position they could see the entire reception hall.

Parker and Ewan were of the same opinion as Hubert Gough and, though they were outwardly in good form as they greeted one another, they were quite firm in their attitudes and were indifferent as to whether or not they returned to their positions in the army. They were adamant that they would not be exposed to the situation that had been forced upon them by Paget and they were, under no condition, prepared to under-take war in Ulster.

At 10.15 hours Hubert Gough was separated from the other officers and led by an orderly into Adjutant General Ewart's waiting room. After a few moments, he was shown into Ewart's office. There, Gough found Ewart seated behind a large desk with Major General Macready standing near the window. Adjutant General Ewart politely asked Gough to sit down and said this was a very grave business, to which Gough replied very sharply, 'I am fully aware of that.'

Gough's manner expressed his feelings. He was very stiff and was determined that under no circumstances would he submit to any form of lecture. He was fully conscious of having committed no offence, and equally conscious that a most cruel and hard position had been forced upon him and the other officers by the War Office and Paget. Ewart said he merely wanted to establish the facts. He asked if Gough thought that any officer had the right to question where he should go in support of a civil power that was there to maintain law and order. Gough retorted, 'None whatever', but he added that he had never been ordered by Sir Arthur Paget to support the civil power. He claimed he had been offered two alternatives and he had accepted one. Gough believed that the army was being used as a pawn in a political game and that the officers were being forced into a precarious position. Gough was ordered to remain in London.

Ewart later wrote of his meetings with the officers in his diary:

> *I saw them one by one, Macready taking notes. They all told the same story, and I came to the conclusion that Paget must be mad. All the officers spoke in the most nice and soldier like way, and said that, if the Brigade had been ordered to Belfast, they would have gone like one man, and would have done all they could to have preserved order, but they understood Paget to mean that the Government had decided to commence hostilities against the Ulstermen but had offered them in the first instance a choice of resigning their commissions in prefer-ence to taking part in the operations. They thought the choice was a hard one, but given it as they believed officially, they preferred of the two courses offered to resign their commissions. There was nothing whatever unsoldier-like about their actions.*[53]

On leaving the War Office, Gough realised that he had started on one of the most difficult and dangerous tasks he had ever undertaken but he knew he had to continue.

---

53 Diary of John Spencer Ewart, 22 March 1914.

As he was departing, he met Major General Sir Henry Wilson. Wilson encouraged the Gough brothers to stand firm and that they were right in refusing to march on Ulster. He urged Gough to demand a written guarantee that the army would not be used to coerce Ulster into accepting Home Rule. Later that afternoon, Gough was ordered to report to the War Office at 11.00 hours the following day.

That evening, Asquith and the senior officers of the army realised that Paget's address to the men of the Curragh had not been inspired by any orders or directions received from the War Office. The Prime Minister wanted the situation sorted as soon as possible because everyone realised that the government was in a precarious position. It was imperative that the army and the government got Gough and his officers to withdraw their resignations and return to their commands immediately.

Asquith was called upon to explain in Parliament why he had been so economical in his handling of the facts. That Sunday night and Monday morning, Asquith was preoccupied with trying to ensure that Gough and his colleagues returned to their duties without further delay and without any further upset within the ranks. Reports from the War Office were sent to Asquith, who now realised that Paget's handling of the case had been anything but proper. The address Paget had given to his officers gave them reason to protest, though they had not refused to obey a formal order. If anything, they had been offered a very confusing and unacceptable set of terms.

Chapter 9

A Lifetime Guarantee

MONDAY, 23 MARCH

Monday morning, 23 March, at the War Office was hectic. Troops were everywhere, coming and going, on foot, on bicycles, on motorbikes and in cars.

At 11.15 hours Brigadier General Hubert Gough was called in to see Field Marshal French and Adjutant General Ewart. Both officers tried to appease Gough. French began by saying that he was Gough's 'old friend and chief' and that he wished to be trusted. He said he wished for Gough to believe that there had been 'a great misunderstanding'. Gough was still in the same frame of mind as the previous day and his stiff appearance showed that he was in no mood to accept any attempt to appease him.

He retorted, 'There has been no misunderstanding on my part, Sir.' French replied, 'As there has been a misunderstanding you are all to return to your commands as if nothing has happened.' Gough was incensed and said, 'I am quite willing to do that, but such a grave crisis has arisen that neither I nor the officers can return unless we receive definite assurance that we shall not be asked again to enforce on Ulster the present Home Rule Bill.' French stated that he would give that assurance, but Gough demanded it in writing. French asked Gough if his word was 'not good enough'. He added, 'Let's wipe the slate clean and go back to Thursday evening.' Gough refused to leave unless he had a written assurance. A long silence ensued, with Gough keeping his eye firmly fixed on the toe of his boot and listening to the tick of the clock on the mantelpiece. After what seemed like an age, French said, 'Very well, there is nothing for it but to take him before the Secretary of War.'[54]

The three officers marched down the corridor to Seely's office. On the way, French took hold of Gough's arm and said, 'For God's sake, go back and don't make any more difficulties. You don't know how serious all this is. If you don't go back, all the War Office will resign. I have done my best for you. If they had attempted to penalise you, I would have resigned myself.'

After a walk of some distance, they came to Seely's office and knocked on the door. A voice called, 'Enter!' Followed by the others, Gough obeyed. As they entered the room, Gough turned to French and said that he 'was awfully grateful.'[55] Seely, General Macready and Lieutenant General Paget were standing together by the fireplace talking in low tones. They moved from their position towards the middle of the room.

Gough recalled later that Seely's manner was one of extreme hauteur. He greeted Gough with an insolent glare and

54 Ryan A.P. *Mutiny At The Curragh*, p. 152-153.
55 Ryan A.P. *Mutiny At The Curragh*, p. 152-153.

haughtily pointed to various chairs and directed the officers to be seated. Gough was surprised at the submissive attitudes of French, Paget and Macready. Seely sat at the head of the table; on his right sat French. Gough took the chair next to French. Paget, Ewart and Macready sat on the opposite side of the table facing Gough.

Colonel Seely immediately turned on Gough and tried to brow beat him by staring. Gough stared back until Seely dropped his gaze. Seely reiterated what French had said in his office. He began to explain the relation of the military to the civil power and that the civil power was justified in using force in order to keep the peace. Gough recognised that Seely's speech was taken almost verbatim from the *Manual of Military Law*. A heated argument ensued between the officers with Gough again insisting that he wanted written assurance that the army would not be used to enforce Home Rule in Ulster. In an attempt to diffuse the situation, French expostulated that 'Perhaps General Gough had not made it quite clear that he feels that he will not be able to reassure his officers or regain their confidence unless he can show them the authority of the Army Council; and that he feels that his own verbal assurance will not be sufficient now that feelings have been so greatly aroused.' Seely immediately grabbed at this chance. Turning to Paget, he said, 'I see. I think that is the only reasonable request.'[56] General Macready was asked to write up a draft that would be presented to Cabinet for approval. The first three paragraphs that were approved read:

---

56 Ryan A.P. *Mutiny At The Curragh*, p. 152-153.

You are authorized by the Army Council to inform the officers of the 3rd Cavalry Brigade that the Army Council are satisfied that the incident which has arisen in regard to their resignations has been due to a misunderstanding.

It is the duty of all soldiers to obey lawful commands given to them through the proper channel by the Army Council, either for the protection of public property and the support of the civil power in the event of disturbances, or for the protection of the lives and property of the inhabitants.

This is the only point it was intended to put to the officers in the questions of the General Officer Commanding, and the Army Council have been glad to learn from you that there never has been and never will be any question of disobeying such lawful orders.[57]

The draft was sent to Cabinet, which, having discussed the paper, broke up and returned the document to Seely, who had not been present at the parliamentary meeting. On reading the document, Seely realised that the terms and conditions that Gough had demanded were not included in the paper. He realised that Gough would not accept this and relayed this to Lord Morley, the Lord President of the Council. Seely believed, and Morley concurred, that Seely had the discretion to change the document without consulting with Cabinet. He decided to add two further paragraphs:

His Majesty's Government must retain their right to use all the forces of the crown in Ireland, or elsewhere, to maintain law and

---

57 Ryan, A.P., *Mutiny at the Curragh*, Macmillan & Co. Ltd, London, 1956, p. 154.

order and to support the civil power in the ordinary execution of its duty.

But they have no intention whatever of taking advantage of the right to crush political opposition to the policy or principles of the Home Rule Bill.[58]

Brigadier General Gough was ordered to return to the War Office at 16.00 hours to sign the document. On receiving the paper, Gough requested fifteen minutes to examine its contents.

French said that the King was waiting for an answer and wanted the problem resolved as soon as possible.

Gough was accompanied by his brother John. Colonel Henry Wilson also joined the group as they pored over the document. Gough read the draft and stated that the paperwork was not acceptable as the phrase 'crush political opposition' could have more than one meaning. He wanted the phrase clearly defined in order to protect himself and his men from being forced to wage war against Ulster.

Gough returned to French's office, taking his fellow officers MacEwan and Parker to act as witnesses to what was being said and implied. Gough entered the room and immediately confronted Ewart and French and stated what he believed the final phrase of the document meant. He posed the following question to the two senior officers: 'In the event of the present Home Rule Bill becoming law, can we be called upon to enforce it on Ulster under the expression of maintaining law and order?'[59]

---

58 Ryan, *Mutiny at the Curragh*, p. 154.
59 Ryan, Mutiny at the Curragh, p. 155.

Gough required a categorical assurance that the answer to this question was in the negative. French became very agitated and paced the room, wringing his hands and considering Gough's request. After a few moments he muttered awkwardly, 'That seems all right.' He walked over to the table, sat down and, under Gough's signature, wrote, 'This is how I read it, J.F.'[60]

Satisfied, Gough bade farewell to the other officers and left the War Office to catch the night mail boat to Ireland.

Seely had added to a cabinet memorandum which French had endorsed with his initials. The paper had been changed without the wider Cabinet's sanction or knowledge. All the officers had endorsed the paper believing that it had cabinet approval, a factor that would have repercussions for all those who initialled it.

The document, later to be known as 'the Guarantee', was to bring the so-called mutiny of the 3rd Cavalry Brigade to an end. However, it was to have far reaching consequences for those in the Army.

---

60 Ryan, Mutiny at the Curragh, p. 155.

Chapter 10

Fallout

The fallout from the Curragh Incident would reverberate throughout British society. News of the meetings between Gough and the War Office, and 'the Guarantee' was leaked to the press. As the officers' meeting came to an end, the British House of Commons erupted into a series of furious debates.

The government rejected 'the Guarantee' on the grounds that the parties who amended the document had no authority to change it. It sought a return of the document from Gough, but to no avail. What Gough had dictated and French's endorsement of it amounted to what many believed was a claim that would place the government and the country at the mercy of the army.

In Parliament, the opposition attacked the government for trying to use the country's armed forces to provoke loyal Ulstermen to a violent confrontation in which they would have been shot down in their thousands. The government benches raised the question of the 'playboy cavalry soldiers' and their 'devil-may-care' attitude. How had they allowed their political views to overshadow their sense of duty and what had occurred to cause the complete breakdown of discipline within the ranks? Accusations flew across the Commons as prominent Conservative Arthur Balfour accused Prime Minister Asquith of coercion against Ulster. Conservative leader Andrew Bonar Law came with letters from serving officers stating that more than just protective measures had been planned against Ulster. However, many of the opposition believed that the planned troop movements against Ulster were part of a carefully planned plot against the province. Conservatives believed that the whole affair had been an elaborate plot by the Liberals to coerce the UVF into firing the first shots, giving the government the excuse to quell the organisation. Winston Churchill was singled out as being the villain of the whole affair. Balfour wrote:

They seem to have made an extraordinary mess over this army matter, and very unnecessarily to have precipitated a crisis which might otherwise, perhaps, never occurred. This is very bad for them and I am afraid it is not very good for the army.

I know no gossip. One story, which you may believe or not as you like, is that this military difficulty is due to Winston, in one of his Napoleonic moods, drawing up a scheme for so encircling Ulster with a military and naval force, that it could be, as it were, strangled into submission. The proposed movement of troops which has led to all these resignations was designed to be the first stage of this operation. The story goes that Asquith was dragged out of bed at half past one on Friday morning to listen to this plan – a reluctant and sleepy assent extracted from him, and orders given in consequence which have led to all the subsequent trouble.[61]

61 Arthur Balfour to Leo Amery, 24 March 1914, Balfour Papers, Add Mss 49863, British Library, London.

On 25 March, *The Times* ran its lead story under the headline 'The Plot that Failed',[62] which referred to Churchill's supposed plan to subdue Ulster. Though the rumours continued, nothing could be proved that implicated Churchill as the instigator of the affair.

Bonar Law demanded a judicial enquiry, which Asquith refused. There was uproar in the Commons with Unionists shouting, 'We want your statement on oath' and 'Will the Prime Minister kindly tell us why, if there is nothing to be ashamed of, he objects to having the truth tested where the statements are given on oath and can be established?'[63] In answer to this question, Asquith slammed his hand down on the despatch box and vehemently exclaimed, 'That, Sir, is an imputation against the honour of ministers.' This heated exchange did not deter Bonar Law who stood up and stated, 'I have already accused the Prime Minister of making statements which are false and he has refused to take an opportunity of either explaining or withdrawing them.'[64]

Asquith issued two white papers containing more information in relation to the Curragh Incident. The first was widely considered a disaster and few took its conclusions seriously, forcing him to issue a second, fuller paper on the event. Both of these papers were attempts to appease the public and both attempts failed.

Lieutenant General Paget was summoned to London where the government, in their efforts to get some sort of understanding of the events in Ireland, instructed him to release a

---

62 *The Times*, 25 March 1914.

63 Ryan, *Mutiny at the Curragh*, p. 167.

64 Ryan, *Mutiny at the Curragh*, p. 167.

written statement detailing the series of events and his involvement. The statement read as follows:

After receiving the instruction of the Secretary of State for War, on the 19th March, I returned at once to Dublin and summoned a conference to meet at 10.00 a.m. on the 20th March.

This conference was attended by the General Officers commanding the 5th Division, 13th and 14th infantry Brigades, 3rd Cavalry Brigade, and by two of my own Staff officers, viz, the Major General in charge of Administration, and the Brigadier-General, General Staff. The officer commanding No.11 District was also present.

I explained to these officers that I had received orders to carry out certain moves of a precautionary nature. The Government believed that the precautionary nature of these moves would be understood, and that they would be carried out without resistance. I said that I personally did not share that opinion, and that I thought that the moves would create intense excitement, and that the country – and if not the country, then the Press – would be ablaze on the following day. I said that the moves might possibly lead to opposition, and might even eventuate, and in the near future, in the taking of active operations against organised bodies of Ulster Volunteer Force under their responsible leaders.

No notes were taken at the conference, and I cannot quote the exact words used, but such was the general impression which I wished to convey, and which as a fact I did convey to the six officers whom I subsequently questioned.

I stated that I had been in close consultation with the War Office on the previous evening and had endeavoured to obtain concessions for those officers who might feel deeply on the subject. The most that I had been able to obtain from Colonel Seely, and that only at a late hour, and by the help of Sir John French, was the following:

Officers actually domiciled in Ulster would be exempted from taking part in any operation that might take place. They would be permitted to 'disappear' (that being the exact phrase used by the War Office) and when all was over would be allowed to resume their places without their career or position being affected.

In answer to a question put to me I said that other officers who were not prepared from Conscientious or other reasons, to carry out their duty, would be dismissed from the Service at once. I said that Colonel Seely had expressed the hope that there would be very few cases of officers claiming exemption.

I said that, as regards the Ulster domicile exemption, I should hold Brigadiers personally responsible that no officer should be exempted unless he fulfilled strictly the conditions laid down, and, in answer to one officer who pointed out the difficulty of ascertaining the facts, I said that very great care would have to be exercised, as an officer granting an exemption to an officer not properly qualified to receive it would render himself liable to trial by Court-Martial.

I said that a second conference would be held at 2.00 p.m. on the afternoon, at which I would discuss the details of moves which it might be necessary to make, in case of resistance to the precautionary moves which were then in process of being carried out.

It was, in my opinion, necessary that I should know before that conference was held, whether the senior officers present were of my way of thinking, viz, that duty came before all other considerations.

I therefore said that I could not allow any officers to attend the second conference who did not feel that he could obey the orders given him in the eventuality which I had sketched. Any such officers would be expected to absent himself [sic] from the second conference, and I should know what he meant.

It is, therefore, quite correct that I did insist on knowing the intentions of these seven officers before the eventuality actually arose.

I had no intention, however, of ascertaining the intentions of subordinate officers. My intention was that senior officers present should simply inform those officers subordinate to themselves of the exemption granted, and of the penalty of refusal to obey orders in the case of officers not affected by the exemption clause. I wished particularly to make it clear to officers that they could not simply resign their commissions and retire from the Service, in possession of pensions and without penalty. Three of the officers present understood me completely, but the remaining four officers understood me to mean that any officer who was not prepared from conscientious or other motives, to carry out his duty was to say so, and would be dismissed from the Service.

I do not understand how the misconception arose in all cases, but Brigadier General Forestier Walker (one of the officers who shared the misapprehension) informs me that, not seeing why Colonel Seely should hope that there would be very few cases of officers claiming exemption owing to a domicile in Ulster, he jumped erroneously to the conclusion that I had made a slip in quoting Colonel Seely's remark and that the latter had really meant that he hoped that there would be very few cases of officers who would be dismissed from the Army rather than do their duty.

It is easy to see that from this it would be a natural step to infer that something in the nature of an alternative was to be put to officers.

Be that it may be certain, officers did leave the conference under a wrong impression, and, as a consequence, the majority of officers of the 5th Division were informed that, if they could not claim exemption, and were not prepared, from conscientious or other motives, to do their duty, they were to say so at once, and would be dismissed from the Service.

The officers of the 3rd Cavalry Brigade were informed in the same sense, but with this variation, that I understand they were told that those who were not prepared, from conscientious or other motives, to do their duty, might resign their commissions, but would be dismissed from the Service.

I regret extremely that this misapprehension arose, and I alone am responsible for it.[65]

Paget's statement added little to the information that the opposition had already garnered. They refused to believe Paget's word and that the white paper released by the government contained the full story of events. Tempers flared in the Commons as the opposition accused the government of attempting to cover up fleet and army movements against Ulster. Asquith claimed that Cabinet had given general permission for a battle squadron to be moved but he did not know that this had been acted upon by the First Lord of the Admiralty until he heard about the movement from Churchill himself. Asquith claimed that he

---

65 Beckett, *The Army & the Curragh Incident 1914*, pp. 157–9.

had put a hold on any further naval movements and that any press releases he had issued to *The Times* had been modified. Debates raged in the Commons on 28 and 29 April, when the opposition pressed for a motion of enquiry.

The national press fuelled the two conflicting views of the situation – one, that there had been a plot against Ulster and, two, that the cavalry officers had gone on strike. One reporter wrote:

The men were of the same mind as their officers; the cavalry fed and watered their horses, but refused to parade; the infantry left their rifles in their racks. From Dublin to Cork, officers and men, cavalry, infantry and artillery, with some few exceptions among the officers, were of one mind. Thus by Friday night the British Army at the Curragh had crumbled in the hands of its Commander-in-Chief.[66]

The 'Curragh Mutiny' and the 'Pogrom Plot', as the episode was to become known, was to bitterly divide the nation and dominate the headlines for the coming weeks.

Seely offered his resignation to Asquith who refused it, stating that it was not necessary.

The King was furious with the government and the army, and demanded an explanation from the Prime Minister.

On 24th March 1914, Asquith wrote:

Mr. Asquith, with his humble duty, thinks it right to acquaint Your Majesty at once with acts which have only come fully to light today.

---

66   Fergusson, *The Curragh Incident*, p. 200.

The letter to be addressed by the Army Council to General Gough was carefully considered and settled by the cabinet yesterday; and it was not until the debate in the House was over that Mr. Asquith was shown a copy of the letter actually delivered, which contained a paragraph – added on his own authority by Colonel Seely of which the Cabinet had never approved and which they would almost certainly have disapproved.

This is the paragraph which is described in today's press as a 'written assurance' that troops will in no case be used for the 'coercion' of Ulster.

Further, Mr. Asquith and his colleagues did not learn until this afternoon that General Gough had yesterday morning in a letter addressed to the Adjutant General demanded such an assurance.

It is impossible for the cabinet to condone the course which has been taken, and it will be their duty to give a full explanation in the House of Commons tomorrow.

In the view of the cabinet, it was wrong to demand from the officers any assurance as to what their conduct might be in a contingency which might never arise, and it is at least equally wrong for an officer to demand any such assurance from the Government.

Their position in the matter was clearly and publicly stated in both Houses yesterday, and the Officers were entitled to nothing more.[67]

Paget also wrote to the King on 25th March 1914, to explain the situation and the actions that he had taken:

67 Beckett, *The Army and the Curragh Incident 1914*, p. 222.

With reference to the audience granted me on the 23rd instant by Your Majesty, and the debate in the House of Commons on the same day, a report of which I have just received, I think it my duty to place before Your Majesty, a short statement of the circumstances that led up to this debate; circumstances which culminated in a garbled account being given to Your Majesty [of what] I said to my senior officers last Friday.

Some weeks ago I reported verbally to the Secretary of State for War and to the Prime Minister that, in view of the political unrest in the country, certain of my depots containing arms and ammunition were practically unguarded, and might easily be raided, and were, in any case, a source of temptation.

On the 15th March I received a letter from the War Office, directing me to take immediate steps to safeguard Depots and other places where stores were kept.

I at once initiated steps to remove reserve arms and ammunition from the more isolated spots, and, in a letter forwarded to the War Office on the 17th instant, I pointed out that, from the point of view of safety, it would be advisable to provide special guards at certain points. I expressed, however, my opinion that such movements of troops would cause intense excitement in Ulster, and might possibly precipitate a crisis; and that therefore I did not consider myself justified in moving troops at that juncture.

On the 18th March, in obedience to a telegraphic summons, I interviewed the Secretary of State for War, and reported to him verbally in the sense of the above letter. I received orders from him to despatch at once the guards which I had recommended for safety reasons, and I sent a cipher instructions from England to carry out the moves, for which orders had been previously drafted before I left Dublin. These moves were to be completed by the early morning of the 21st March.

I received no other orders from the War Office, except to return and take whatever action I thought right to maintain law and order, in the event of any of my troops, then on the move by road and rail, meeting with opposition.

Holding, as I did, the opinion that the movement of troops which had been ordered might precipitate a crisis, I considered it necessary to summon an immediate conference of senior officers, since I was not certain that all my Brigadiers were of my own opinion that duty came before any consideration. Had any of my senior officers refused to obey or act in the circumstances which, in my opinion, might arise at very short notice, the results would have been even more serious than the present position. I knew that all troops were loyal to the sovereign, but I had doubts as to their loyalty to His Advisers.

This Conference, which was attended by the General Officer Commanding 5th Division, and the Brigadier-Generals of the Cavalry Brigade, and the 13th and 14th Infantry Brigades, was held at 10.00 a.m. on the morning of the 20th instant.

I informed the officers that I had received orders to carry out certain movements of troops, and that the Secretary of State of War had assured me that these movements were only in support of law and order. I told the officers, however, that though these movements were in themselves undoubtedly in support of law and order, I was of the opinion that they would cause great excitement, and that possibly there might be opposition. In the latter case I must be prepared to move at once to the support of my troops, and that a situation might then rapidly evolve which might set Ireland ablaze by Saturday, and would lead to something more serious than quelling local disturbances.

I then informed the officers that, in view of the possibility of active operations in Ulster, the War Office had authorized me to make the following communication to officers:

Officers whose names were actually in the province of Ulster might, if they wished to do so, apply for permission to be absent from duty during the period of operations, and would be allowed to disappear from Ireland. Such officers would be subsequently reinstated and would suffer no loss in their career.

I added that any officer who, from conscientious or other motives, were not prepared to carry out his duty should say so, and in answer to a question, I said 'such officers will at once be dismissed from the Service.' I expressed the hope that very few cases would be found of officers who elected thus to sever their connection with the Service.

As regards the exemption offered to officers whose homes were in Ulster, the limitation was to be interpreted strictly and literally. I explained to the assembled officers that it would be necessary to hold a Conference in the afternoon, in order to explain possible developments and my plans, and that no officer could be allowed to attend this Conference who did not mean to carry out the orders given to him. Consequently, any officer present who had doubts as to his conduct must decide before 2.00 p.m. I then asked if any officer present wished to make any remark.

Brigadier General Gough then explained his own position, and stated that he could not claim exemption as a resident of Ulster,

*but that on account of birth and upbringing, and many friend-
ships, he did not see how he could bear arms against the Ulster
Loyalists, and that, if he did take up arms against them, he could
never face his friends again.*

*I informed General Gough that no exception could be made in his
case, that he must consider his position seriously, and that I hoped
I should see him at the second Conference.*

*The Conference then broke up, and General Gough did not attend
the second Conference in the afternoon.*

*On hearing late that day that a number of officers of the 3rd
Cavalry Brigade intended to resign, I went down on the following
morning to the Curragh and, to save the reputation of these
three regiments and the credit of the forces in Ireland, I made
certain concessions of which I have already informed Your Majesty
verbally, which I did not think that they could possibly refuse. I
cannot hold myself justified in making these concessions, but had
General Gough and his officers trusted me and withdrawn their
resignations, the critical situation with regard to the Army, as
disclosed by the debate in the House of Commons last Monday,
would never have taken place.*[68]

Officers other than Paget were also reeling from the fallout of
the Curragh Incident. After addressing his men and encouraging them not to resign, Major General Fergusson found
himself in trouble with the King and with Parliament. Lord
Stamfordham wrote to Fergusson stating that the King was
much disturbed by a letter he had received from an infantry

68 Beckett, *The Army and the Curragh Incident 1914*, p. 120.

colonel that stated that he had given his men the assurance of the Commander-in-Chief, Paget, that what had been ordered had been fully approved by his Majesty. The letter included the phrase 'The King has given the order and we one and all obeyed.'

Fergusson defended his actions by writing to Stamfordham explaining that he had been deceived and had, in turn, deceived his men. He had acted under the impression that he was carrying out the orders of His Majesty. He further stated that he would tender his resignation over the incident. On hearing of Fergusson's offered resignation, the King sent a telegram to the officer telling him 'most certainly do nothing'.

On the other hand, Brigadier General Gough and the other officers returned to the Curragh as heroes. A two-horse carriage awaited the officers as they arrived at the train station. As they prepared to leave, fifty lancers in review order rode up. The horses were taken away and a four-horse team was substituted, with two lancers as postillions. The remaining troopers formed an escort and rode before and behind the carriage. All ranks turned out to cheer the group as they entered the camp. As the carriage came to a halt outside the Cavalry Brigade Headquarters, a large group gathered closely around the vehicle. Gough addressed the men with a few words, stating that even though they were soldiers they had the same rights as other men and had a right to follow the dictates of their conscience. The men cheered as Gough and the others retired to their quarters.

Gough immediately contacted his solicitor in Dublin and organised that a trust deed be drawn up that handed over the signed guarantee to his eldest daughter Myrtle, 'her heirs and successors for ever'.[69] Gough believed that the government would look for the guarantee to be returned, which they did. Gough told them to ask the trustee but the government never pursued this line of enquiry.

As Gough returned to his command, he tried to sink back into the obscurity that he claimed was provided by his work as a soldier.[70] He received many letters and telegrams of support from people in Ireland and Britain. He also received letters from people who condemned his actions and accused him of treasonable behaviour that was not fitting for an officer of the Crown.

Gough secretly remained sceptical of Sir Henry Wilson's involvement in the Curragh Incident. A month after the crisis, Gough told General Alex Godley that Wilson 'talked a lot about resigning, etc., previously, but never raised a finger till everyone else did. He was however useful in various ways but did not mean to risk his own skin, and was very glad to help us pull out the chestnuts for him.'[71]

On 26 March the editorial of the *Morning Post* stated, 'The Army has killed the Home Rule Bill, and the sooner the government recognises the fact the better.'

The officers who had stood in the War Office on 23 March and had argued over the Curragh Incident couldn't have known that they would find themselves destined to meet again, five months later, in very different circumstances. While some of the officers had parted on good terms after the incident, others harboured feelings of antagonism. However, these feelings

---

69 Gough, *Soldiering On*, p. 110.
70 Gough, *Soldiering On*, p. 110.
71 Gough, *Soldiering On*, p. 172.

would have to be put aside as they became united under one aim – the defence of the British Isles in the Great War.

In the House of Commons, Asquith stated that the government would never give in to the demands of anyone in the service of the Crown as to what they would or would not do in circumstances that had not even arisen.

The situation had become the talking point throughout British and Irish society, not least when Field Marshal French and Adjutant General Ewart resigned. However, this was not the end. There was to be one more resignation.

Chapter 11

Dismissed

Secretary of State for War J. E. B. Seely's second offer of resignation was accepted by the Prime Minister and Parliament. In the House of Commons Seely stated that he tendered his resignation in order that it might not appear that a minister of the Crown had made a bargain with any of the Crown's servants as to the terms of service under which they should serve. Seely attempted to defend the actions of Field Marshal French and implored that the army should retain the services of what he called 'our most brilliant living soldier'. He finished his address by saying that, though he was resigning from his ministerial post, he was retaining his position in Parliament, and that he hoped the House believed him when he stated that he had tried to serve Parliament faithfully and to see fair play in his dealings with the British army at a difficult time.[72]

In the House of Commons, Asquith stated:

Field Marshal Sir John French and General Sir Spencer Ewart both intimated their wish to retire, not because of any difference

---

72 Hansard, House of Commons, April 1914.

between their view and that of the government as to the conditions under which the army serves or should be employed in aid of the civil power, but because, having initialled the Memorandum which had been published, and which, as the House knows, had been handed to General Gough, they thought that course incumbent upon them. That is the ground and the sole ground of their retirement.[73]

Asquith became his own war minister, declaring that 'the army will hear nothing of politics from me and, in return, I expect to hear nothing of politics from the army.'[74] Army command had been shaken to its very foundations and the relationship between the army and the government had been shattered.

Asquith's first task was to restore order in the armed forces. Sir Charles Douglas was appointed Chief of the Imperial General Staff in place of French and Sir Henry Slater took over the position of Adjutant General from Ewart. These appointments were the beginning of a long and arduous road that sought to repair the relationship between the government and the army.

In response to the Curragh Incident, Asquith issued a new army order on 27 March 1914:

1. No officer or soldier shall in future be questioned by his superior as to the attitude he will adopt, or as to his action, in the event of his being required to obey orders dependent upon future or hypothetical contingencies.

2. An officer or soldier is forbidden in future to ask for assurances as to the orders which he may be required to carry out.

---

73 Bodleian, Ms Asquith 7, f109.
74 Ryan, *Mutiny at the Curragh*, p. 159.

3. In particular, it is the duty of every officer and soldier to obey all lawful commands given to them through the proper channel, either for the safe-guarding of public property or the support of the civil power in the ordinary execution of its duty, or for the protection of the lives and property of the inhabitants in the case of the disturbance of the peace.[75]

The Curragh Incident still remained in the newspaper headlines, and many continued to believe that it had been a Liberal plot to force Ulster into civil disobedience, which the military would then put down. Colonel Harvey, the historian of the 5th Lancers, later wrote on the incident:

Thus ended this historic event, in which Colonel A. Parker, commanding the 5th Lancers, and the other commanding officers of the 3rd Cavalry Brigade, as well as the Brigadier Commander, were exonerated for the noble and patriotic part they had shared with the other officers of the Brigade in declining to participate in a coup d'etat of an unscrupulous Government and which would have involved British soldiers in the most despicable duties that they could possibly have been asked to perform.

For the attitude adopted by the officers of the 5th Lancers, and their other comrades in the 3rd Cavalry Brigade, and to which they were set an example by their commanding officers, they ought to be blazoned in letters of gold, and thus transmitted to history.[76]

---

75 Beckett, *The Army and the Curragh Incident 1914*, p. 344.

76 Harvey, Colonel J. S., *History of the 5th Royal Irish Lancers, 1858–1919*, National Army Museum, London, 1924, p. 168.

No proof ever emerged that there was any conspiracy by the army or Parliament to coerce Ulster into Home Rule or to subdue the UVF using the armed forces of Britain. However, there were those who would have liked to see Asquith's Liberal government fall. Sir Henry Wilson wrote in his diary that 'the disclosure of these orders ... will ruin Winston, Lloyd George, Birrell, Seely and Asquith.' He continued, 'We soldiers beat Asquith and his vile tricks.'[77]

The Curragh Incident contributed both to the Unionist and Nationalist separatist movements, convincing Nationalists that they could not expect support from the British army in Ireland and assuring Unionists that the military would not intervene in any action they intended to take.

Intelligence reports from Ireland stated that the situation in Belfast and elsewhere in the country was peaceful. A section of Field Company and a detachment of the Army Service Corps, which had been sent to reinforce the troops at Holywood in county Down, had arrived without incident. The army still possessed doubts about many of its units refusing to fight if war erupted in Ulster. If martial law had to be imposed in the province, Lieutenant General Paget stated that, though the Royal Irish Constabulary would come under military control, he could not rely on the Inspector General of that force as he considered him lacking in character and initiative. The War Office was very concerned with the threats posed by some of its gentlemen rankers. Parliament eyed them with suspicion, not knowing if they could be trusted to act when circumstances demanded it.

---

77 Callwell, *Field Marshall Sir Henry Wilson, His Life and Diaries*, vol. 1, pp. 142,146.

Many people believed that the government and the army had mishandled the situation and that Gough and the military should not have been put in such a position.

Field Marshal Lord Grenfell wrote:

The crisis was entirely owing to the criminal folly of the Government in allowing Ulster to organise a force for over a year, attempting by derision to minimize the danger which they dared not face....
In a gossip I had with Lord Cromer, he said that he considered that the bungling and evasive policy of the Government, putting hypothetical questions to officers of the Curragh, proved that the Government was absolutely incompetent to deal with such a question as that on which the crisis was based.[78]

However, there were those who felt that orders were orders and that they should be obeyed; it was not a soldier's duty to question a direct order.

The King was furious with the whole affair and remarked to Ewart that Paget had made a mess out of it. He was also unhappy at the idea that Paget had tried to get the officers at the Curragh to carry out their duties in the King's name. An immediate enquiry was launched to see if Paget had used the King's name. Interviews with officers revealed that they all had the unmistakable impression that the instructions Paget relayed to them had been approved by the King. However, a statement issued on 29 June by Major General Fergusson clarified who had brought the King's name into the address:

---

78 Grenfell, Lord F. W.), *Memoirs of Field Marshall Lord Grenfell, London, Hodder & Stoughton*, 1925, p. 202.

On Friday March 20, I asked the G O C-in-Chief whether certain orders were the King's, or had his Majesty's sanction (I am not sure of the exact words used). He replied in the affirmative.

At the time I had in my mind the idea of ascertaining whether the orders actually had His Majesty's sanction and approval, and it was in that sense that I put the question. I interrupted the answer in the same sense.

Consequently, when next morning I was questioned by officers, I first replied (speaking in the technical sense) that of course the orders were from the King. This, however, did not satisfy them; and on being pressed by them as to whether the orders actually had His Majesty's sanction, I answered that I had put the same question to the G O C-in-Chief, and that he had replied 'yes'.

On consideration I admit freely that my question might easily have been misunderstood, and that the answer of the G O C-in-Chief would apply equally to the question in its technical meaning. No doubt our minds at the moment were running in different grooves.

The Commander-in-Chief never mentioned the King's name at all, except in answering the specific question I put to him. Nor did I use it, until cornered by the questioning of officers, when I thought that under the circumstances there was no alternative if a catastrophe was to be avoided.

I am entirely to blame for the introduction of His Majesty's name. It was I who first introduced it, and I am responsible for the use made of it.[79]

---

79   R A GVF. 674/93; Fergusson Mss; BL Add Mss 51250, Paget Mss.

Fergusson's admission brought some relief to those angered by the use of the King's name, but the incident still remained the topic of conversation.

On 21 May the Home Rule Bill came up for its third reading and was shouted down by the opposition. The Curragh Incident and the possibility of Home Rule for Ireland were the main topics of conversation in London society:

> *The battle raged furiously through London, where people dined against each other in the deadliest fashion, and where drawing-room met drawing-room in mortal combat. This singular warfare, with its accompanying rattle of cutlery and popping of wine corks, grew in intensity as the season advanced. Entrenched behind acres of flowers and miles of table linen, hostesses gave battle; rival orchestras moaned and thundered through the nights; on neutral ground, there were constant exchanges of snubs and shrugs and cuts direct.*[80]

Speeches made by politicians added fuel to the fire. A speech, condemning the Army and the actions of its officers, given by Labour leader J. Ramsay MacDonald received the following response by Major A. W. F. Baird of the 1st Gordon Highlanders:

> *I have just been reading the report of a speech delivered by you at Newcastle on Tyne on Apl. 24th.*
>
> *I do not know to what extent you have studied the King's Regulations, but judging from the blackguardly assertions made in your speech, it seems safe to assume that you are well aware of the*

---

80 Beckett, *The Army and the Curragh Incident 1914*, p. 370.

paragraph which protects you from any chance of a public reply by an Army officer.

Nothing, however, prevents my writing to you privately. I therefore do so to inform you, that I for one, and hundreds of others of all ranks in the service, detest you and all other politicians of all classes and denominations equally.

In our opinion you are all tarred with the same brush. Your personal interests and your party interests, in so far as the latter coincide with the former (and your £400 a year makes the coincidence wonderfully accurate no doubt!) are all that any of you care for. The King, Empire and the Flag which are everything to us are little or nothing to any of you.

In stating publicly that those of us in the service (and there are many of us) who would sooner sacrifice, than dishonour, our careers, are influenced in our decision by the views or advice of any political party, you are stating either a deliberate or an unintentional falsehood. Moreover no one but a blackguard or a politician would make such a statement, knowing, as you must have done, that there was no chance of any public reply. In case you may contemplate making any further public speeches on this subject, perhaps you will be good enough to mention that you have heard directly from at least one officer on the active list that he is prepared to sacrifice his career, his prospects, and his pay (small as it is compared to your own) rather than take up arms against Ulster and that the motive of his action has nothing whatsoever to do with Tory politicians, but it is based on his conscientious belief that the leaders of the Nationalists of Ireland are at heart just as much rebels to our King and our Country today as they have openly and repeatedly proclaimed themselves to be until quite recently. I must add that, not being a trade unionist, I should not consider it right, in the event of my resigning my commission, to adopt any system of 'peaceful picketing' with regard to those who might differ from me, as I have never seen any justification for bullying the wives and families of those who may desire to continue in their employment.[81]

The fallout from Curragh Incident continued to be felt in the months that followed, and there was a lot of bad blood among the military hierarchy and politicians. Major General Sir Henry Wilson had watched closely the series of events as they unfolded. Once he felt that the immediate crisis had passed, his concerns moved on from the danger of the army splitting to the political advantages which could be accrued from the situation.

---

81 PRO 30/69/1423, Macdonald Mss.

Chapter 12

The Guns of Ulster

Unknown to the authorities, the Ulster Volunteer Force had sent agents to Europe to procure weapons and ammunition. These arms and ammunition would be used to secure and protect a provisional government, whose job it would be to ensure that the political status of the counties of Ulster would remain unchanged.

Throughout 1913 Major Frederick H. Crawford and Captain Wilfrid Spender, with the use of aliases and disguises, had attempted to smuggle arms and ammunition into Ulster that they purchased in Britain and Germany. However, these attempts were thwarted by government officials and the Royal Navy. One attempt to land guns at Carrigart in northern Donegal ended in failure as the shipment was intercepted by naval patrol boats.

Undeterred, Crawford and Spender convinced the Ulster Unionist Council that they could provide all the weapons and ammunition that would be needed to equip the UVF. They were permitted to continue their mission. Edward Carson proclaimed, 'I'll see you though this business, if I should have to go to prison for it.' If the mission was to succeed, they would have to come up with a plan that would enable them to land the munitions and evade capture.

Crawford purchased 216 tonnes of weapons from Benny Spiro, an arms dealer based in Hamburg, Germany. The weapons included 11,000 Mannlicher rifles, 9,000 ex-German army Mauser rifles, 4,600 Italian Vetterli rifles and 5 million rounds of ammunition. The ordnance was smuggled out of Hamburg via the Kiel Canal to the Danish island of Langeland. As the arms were being loaded on to the ship *SS Fanny*, Danish custom officials seized the ship's papers. However, the ship managed to slip out of port under the cover of a gale and, evading the Danish navy, sailed towards Ireland.

Crawford now began the second phase of his plan. He had purchased another ship, the *SS Clyde Valley*, and on 19–20 April 1914, off the County Wexford coast at Tusker Rock, Crawford's crew transported the entire cargo of weapons from one ship to another. Three days later, as the ship sailed northwards, the crew changed the name of the vessel from the *SS Clyde Valley* to the *Mountjoy II*. Using six-foot-long canvas strips, with the words *Mountjoy II* written in white lettering on a black background, the ship was renamed. This ruse was not only to deceive the authorities but was also a direct reference to the ship, the *Mountjoy*, which had managed to cross the boom that blocked the River Foyle in 1689 and relieve the siege of Derry City. Once again, Crawford and his crew would evade the blockade of the coast and deliver their cargo.

On 24 April, General Sir William Adair of the UVF Motor Corps was summoned by the County Antrim UVF Commander and given the following orders:

> *It is absolutely necessary that your cars should arrive at Larne in the night of Friday/Saturday 24th–25th instant at 1 a.m. punctually but not before the hour for a very secret and important duty.*[82]

UVF members were mobilised to take part in what many believed was an exercise. Only twelve members knew the real reasons behind the mobilisation and the deployment of their forces. Units tapped and cut telephone lines into Larne while others manned pickets that controlled access and egress into their area of operations. The roads between Larne and Belfast were covered by patrols that also secured the towns of Ballyclare, Ballymena and Glenarm. The cordon around Larne would only permit those with special passes to enter or leave the town.

The operation in Bangor was commanded by Captain James Craig while General Sir William Adair took charge at Larne. The Commander of the UVF Sir George Richardson would remain in Belfast, where he would be kept fully informed of the operation by dispatch riders. As zero hour approached, each commander knew that if the authorities got wind of the operation there could be an armed confrontation that could result in bloodshed.

In order to draw the authorities away from the designated landing areas, an elaborate hoax was devised by the UVF. They would sail the tramp steamer *SS Balmerino* into Belfast Lough as a decoy for the authorities. To add to the charade, a truck would also be waiting on the dockside. The authorities were immediately alerted to the suspicious activities in Belfast Lough and

---

82 Lewis, *Carson: The Man Who Divided Ireland*, p. 107.

Harbour. As the *SS Balmerino* docked, it was boarded by custom officials. Arguments ensued between the captain of the ship and port authorities who believed the ship was carrying arms. When the hatches of the mysterious collier were opened, it materialised that the holds were full of coal. The captain of the ship had delayed the authorities throughout the night, stalling for precious time as the real operation was taking place just twenty miles away.

At Larne Harbour, the *Mountjoy II* docked unhindered. A motor launch pulled up alongside and, with the use of a crane, hundreds of boxes of rifles and ammunition were unloaded. Another vessel arrived and the scene was repeated. Both launches sailed away towards Donaghadee. Units of men worked through the night unloading the weapons from the boats and moving them by motor vehicles to designated arms dumps in the surrounding areas. *The Belfast Evening Telegraph* later reported:

> *There was no rush or bustle in the doing of it. It was accomplished with celerity, yet without fuss or splutter, because it was done in pursuance of a well-formed plan, executed as perfectly as it had been preconceived. So exactly had this mobilisation been arranged that these hundreds of motors reached the assembly point at an identical moment. It was an amazing sight to see this huge procession of cars nearly three miles in length descending upon the town with all their headlights ablaze.*[83]

At 05.00 hours the ship set sail from Larne Harbour to Bangor, where the remainder of its cargo was unloaded. By 07.00

---

83 *The Belfast Evening Telegraph*, 28 April 1914.

hours the mission had been completed and the *Mountjoy II* set a course for the River Clyde in order to confuse any naval vessels that may have been shadowing it. The canvas sheets bearing the name the *Mountjoy II* were discarded at sea, revealing the ship's real name, the *SS Clyde Valley*. It sailed down the Irish Sea unhindered, where it briefly stopped at Rosslare in Wexford to offload Major Crawford. The ship then set sail for the Baltic Sea, travelling along the coasts of France and Denmark, where the Ulstermen on board were transferred to another vessel and returned to Ireland.

The UVF had managed to smuggle over 20,000 rifles and 3 million rounds of ammunition into Ulster. The operation had involved people at the highest levels of political, business and commercial life in Ireland and Britain. Defying the British government, all these elements had rallied together in order to oppose against any attempt to enforce Home Rule in Ireland.

Chapter 13

The Calm Before
The Storm

In Ireland, the stand-off between the two armed forces of the Unionist Ulster Volunteer Force and the Nationalist Irish Volunteers continued. A memorandum issued in April 1914 by the military members of the British Army Council on the military situation in Ireland stated:

- *At the present time two opposing forces, with approximately a total strength of 200,000 men, are being systematically and deliberately raised, trained and equipped and organised on a military basis in Ireland.*
- *In view of this fact we, as the responsible military advisers to His Majesty's Government, deem it to be our duty to point out that if, unfortunately, these two large forces should come into conflict, a situation may arise which may require the whole of our available forces at home to deal with.*
- *As we have not been informed what policy the Government proposes to adopt in the event of such a conflict, it is not possible for us to estimate the number of troops which might be required to restore*

order. No plan of operations of this nature has been prepared or even considered by the War Office, and no plan can, in the circumstances, be prepared.

- *We think it likely, however, that it might be necessary to employ the whole of our Expeditionary Force to restore order, and this would probably involve general mobilisation, placing Special Reserve troops in the ports, and assembling the Local and Central Forces now composed of Territorial troops.*

- *So far as numbers alone are concerned, there might be no great difficulty in finding garrisons for the ports or in providing a Central Force, but a factor which cannot be overlooked is that, as the Territorial Force cannot be used to maintain order in Great Britain, we should probably be unable to use the whole of our six divisions in Ireland.*

- *A still more important factor is that, if the whole of our Expeditionary Force were used in Ireland and to maintain order in Great Britain, we should be quite incapable of meeting our obligations abroad. And in this connection India and Egypt must be specially borne in mind. It seems to us at least possible that unrest in India and in Egypt may follow the commencement of such operations, whilst certain countries in Europe may take this opportunity of creating trouble.*

- *We now summarise the chief points to which we wish to call attention –*

    - *No plan for military operations in Ireland of the nature herein questioned has been prepared or even considered by the War Office.*

    - *No plan can be made until the policy which His Majesty's Government proposes to adopt is given.*

    - *In the event of a conflagration in Ireland, the whole of the Expeditionary Force may be required to restore law and order, not only in Ireland but in Great Britain as well.*

- *If the whole of it is required, our Central Force will be inadequate security against invasion; we shall be unable to give any assistance to either Egypt or India; and finally, be unable to meet any of our obligations abroad.*

We trust you will not think that in putting this forward we are making any attempt to interfere in a political question which is outside our province; but as the responsible military advisers of His Majesty's Government we feel we should be neglecting our duty if we omitted to draw attention to the serious aspect of the situation which may arise from a military point of view.[84]

With Ireland apparently on the verge of a civil war, the government had to diffuse the escalating situation. Prime Minister Asquith, at the request of King George V, summoned a meeting at Buckingham Palace. The Buckingham Palace Conference took place between 21 and 24 July 1914 and represented all those groups that were involved in the Home Rule crisis. The Liberals were represented by Asquith and David Lloyd George, with John Redmond and John Dillon legating for the Nationalists. James Craig and Edward Carson were the delegates for the Ulster Unionists. Andrew Bonar Law and Lord Landsdowne 'sat in' for the Conservatives. The main item on the agenda was whether or not part, or all, of Ulster, should be excluded from a Home Rule arrangement. The question of whether the northern province should include the border counties of Fermanagh and Tyrone caused serious debate amongst the candidates. Unable to reach a compromise, the meeting

---

84 PRO, Cab. 37/119/44 W.O. 32/9569; IWM 73/1/17 Wilson Mss.

became deadlocked. Major General Sir Henry Wilson watched the proceedings with avid interest. During most of July 1914, his principal worry was the possibility of civil war in Ireland.

It appeared that Ireland was not to be granted the Home Rule proposed by the Bill of 1912. Irish Nationalists were becoming disillusioned with Redmond and his party. Two days later, this disaffection was to be shown publicly in Ireland.

On 26 July 1914, Erskine Childers captained the yacht the *Asgard* into Howth Harbour in broad daylight. This boat was packed with weapons that were landed and moved to safe houses in Dublin City by The Irish Volunteers. The arms consignment was purchased in Antwerp and consisted of 1,500 Mauser rifles and 45,000 rounds of ammunition. In order to avoid detection by the authorities, yachts were used to smuggle the arms into Ireland. As heavily laden Volunteers moved down Batchelor's Walk along the quays of the River Liffey on their return journey from Howth, a detachment of the King's Own Scottish Borderers (KOSB) attempted to intercept the consignment. After a heated exchange of words with the Volunteers and locals, the KOSB opened fire into the crowd, killing four bystanders and wounding many others. After this incident, many Nationalists believed that a double standard was in action. Those who obeyed the law and acted in support of the government were in danger of being killed while others, and by this they meant the Unionists, who defied the will of Parliament were permitted to import arms and act with impunity. The incident at Batchelor's Walk caused Asquith a lot of embarrassment and heightened the tension in Ireland.

The remainder of the Nationalist consignment was landed in Wicklow in early August. Both the UVF and the Irish

Volunteers had defied the British government and were arming and training for confrontation. In the face of such open resistance, the British government seemed to sit by and watch as Ireland plunged ever nearer civil war.

Within the ranks of the armed forces there was still unrest and suspicion. Brigadier General G. T. Forestier Walker wrote to Major General Fergusson in relation to an incident that occurred while on an exercise.

An incident occurred during the Comd. Exercise, of which I think I ought to inform you. An officer informed me that a paper dealing with political matters was being passed round among the officers assembled for the Exercise. My informant had not himself seen the paper, but I found out who was in possession of it, and I asked the officer for an explanation. He informed me that the paper was intended as a joke and did not bear the significance that I had attributed to it. He said that it had been handed to him in jest by an officer whose name he did not wish to disclose since he now realised that he had done a silly thing in showing the paper about, and he did not wish to embroil the officer concerned. I accepted this explanation, and took it upon myself to give him a very severe telling off, and pointed out the very serious results which might have accrued to himself and others owing to his peculiar ideas on the subject of humour. He gave me his word of honour that he would destroy immediately the paper (which I did not ask to see), and that he would personally make certain that the two or three officers, to whom it had been shown, understood it to be a joke, and further that any officers, to whom the existence of the paper had thereby become known, also understood it in that sense. Later on, he informed me that he had done this.

I reported the matter to the MG/A [Major General, Acting]
yesterday. He considered that the action which I had taken was
sufficient from a disciplinary point of view, and that the matter
may be considered closed. I think and Genl. Friend does too, that
you should know of the incident, because the officer who was in
possession of the paper is one of those under your command, and
it is conceivable, though I hope improbable, that you may hear of it
from other sources. In the hope, however, that the matter is finally
closed, I have not mentioned his name.[85]

Fergusson was livid about the incident and believed that
the culprits should be 'hunted down to the bitter end'.[86] He
believed that no mercy should be shown to officers that were
passing around seditious papers; what incensed him the most
was that it was a staff officer who was inciting this type of
behaviour. Fergusson wrote, 'These fellows think we are afraid
to take any action in the interests of discipline, and that the
public feeling in favour of Gough and his party prevents
anything being said on the other side.' Senior officers still did
not trust the two Curragh battalions of Fergusson's brigade
and Fergusson himself was worried about his junior officers.
Though he accepted that Brigadier General Forestier Walker
had reprimanded the offending officer, Fergusson stated that
'the young gentleman may thank his stars that he didn't fall into
my clutches!'[87]

In many of the commands throughout Ireland and England,
divisional and brigade commanders were addressed on the

85 PRO, WO 35/209 (b).

86 PRO, WO 35/209 (b).

87 PRO, WO 35/209 (b).

moral that was to be drawn from the Curragh Incident. The danger to the Empire caused by the disruption of the army through officers dabbling in politics was firmly explained to all those that assembled. The actions of a few officers had shaken the state to its foundations and if such an incident was to occur again, the Empire, both at home and overseas, would be endangered beyond comprehension.

However, events in Europe were to overshadow the threat of civil war in Ireland. In June, the events in Sarajevo set in train the mobilisations of armed forces in France, Germany, Russia and Britain.

The German threat was a far greater problem for Britain than a civil war in Ireland. The leader of the Irish Parliamentary Party John Redmond was unsure as to whether to pursue his demand for Home Rule and risk a civil war or forego Home Rule until the crisis in Europe had been resolved. After deep deliberation he chose the latter course, and on 3 August he announced in the House of Commons that Britain need not worry about trouble in Ireland. Home Rule was placed on the statute book in the form of a Suspensory Bill that was scheduled to take effect as soon as the war was over. However, the clause also stated that Westminster should be allowed to amend the Home Rule legislation to the satisfaction of the Ulster Unionists.

The assassination of the heir to the Hapsburg throne Archduke Ferdinand plunged Europe into war. His murder provided Austria with the opportunity she wanted to eliminate Serbia. A series of alliances began to to form as Russia came to the assistance of Serbia. Germany issued Russia with an ultimatum: to cease mobilisation forthwith. When this request was ignored, Germany declared war on Russia. Within forty-eight hours Germany would also be at war with France. Germany knew that a war on two fronts would be difficult and called into action the Schlieffen Plan. This plan involved a rapid strike to neutralise the threat from France, after which German forces could turn their full attention to Russia.

Under the Schlieffen Plan, Germany aimed to attack France through Belgium. At this time Belgium was neutral and both Britain and Germany guaranteed that neutrality. The Germans were willing to forget their guarantee in order to launch their attack and defeat France in one swift blow. Calls for Germany to respect Belgium's neutral stance were ignored and, as a consequence, Britain declared war on Germany and its allies on 4 August 1914. The Great War had begun.

On hearing that Britain had declared war on Germany, John Redmond rose in the House of Commons and proclaimed Irish support for the war effort. Though he was applauded in Parliament, the news was not so well received in Ireland. The Irish Volunteers split into two groups: the Irish Volunteers led by Eoin MacNeill, who did not agree with Irish involvement in a European war, and the National Volunteers, who supported Redmond's decision. Redmond attempted to convince a suspicious Secretary of State for War Lord Kitchener that his men should be allowed to enlist and see action together as one division. This was never to happen as many joined the Irish regiments that already existed.

Ulster Unionists had proved that they were willing to fight to preserve the integrity of the United Kingdom of Great Britain and Ireland. The incident at the Curragh as well as the conferences at the War Office, at Aldershot and elsewhere

123

had made it clear that the army would not be used to enforce legislation on Ulster. In early July Sir Douglas Haig's Chief of Staff, General John Gough VC, visited Ulster and stated that the idea of coercion had been abandoned. He mentioned that the Ulster Volunteers could, with experienced and trained leadership, be made into a very formidable fighting force. German forces were now threatening the integrity of the Union and Ulstermen were called upon to support King and Country. Edward Carson was soon in discussions with Kitchener to raise a division to defend the Crown. By September 1914 the 36th Ulster Division had been created and was in training for deployment to the Western Front.

As war was declared, many of those officers that had played key roles in the Curragh Incident rallied to the flag, believing that this war would be their last chance of achieving some form of glory. Little did they know that the forthcoming war would be very different from the colonial wars of their youth and that it would test the relationship between the British government and its army.

Chapter 14

Trial By Fire

A British Expeditionary Force (BEF) of four infantry divisions and one cavalry division, supported by an extra cavalry brigade, would go to war. The force would be commanded by Field Marshal Sir John French; the four infantry divisions that would form I Corp were commanded by Field Marshall, Sir Douglas Haig, and II Corp would be under Lieutenant General, Sir James Grierson. Major General Allenby had command of the cavalry division.

From the outset of operations, Secretary of State for War Lord Kitchener, had little faith in Field Marshal French and distrusted Director of Military Operations Sir Henry Wilson.

At this time there were an estimated 21,000 Irishmen serving in the British army. Another 47,000 reserve officers and men were quickly mobilised in the weeks that followed. Most of these professional soldiers were mobilised on 4 August with the advance parties sailing for France on 7 August. The main elements began their journey on 12 August, with English units leaving from Southampton. Those stationed in Ireland left from Dublin, Cork and Belfast. They were well trained but poorly equipped for the mass war that was coming.

On the outbreak of war, Brigadier General Gough took his brigade to France and was soon in the thick of the action. As German forces swept through Belgium, the BEF was ordered to hold a defensive line along a sixteen-mile length of the Mons-Condé Canal. The town of Mons was the centre of the Belgian coal-mining area, which was dominated by small villages and slag heaps. British forces began to dig in and make ready. Both Haig and the newly appointed General Sir Horace Smith Dorrien were concerned about their ability to hold their positions against the advancing German forces.

At 11.15 hours on Saturday, 22 August one of Gough's artillery batteries, E Battery of the Royal Horse Artillery, fired the first shot of the war against the advancing Germans. Gough's defensive line extended along the Sambre-Oise Canal, east of Mons.[88] Nearby, Field Marshal French held the outer suburbs of Mons.

Gunner Walter Burchmore of the Royal Horse Artillery recalled:

We had reached a village about three miles from Mons in our advance towards the German armies and we were enjoying the hospitality of the villagers when quite out of the blue came the order 'Prepare for Action. Get mounted.' We obeyed it immediately, rode out of the village about a couple of miles. We came into action on the high ground overlooking Mons. We immediately engaged the German artillery and that developed into a regular artillery

---

88 Gough, *Soldiering On.*

duel in and around Binche, where we were firing in support of our infantry and cavalry who occupied it in the early morning. It was quite obvious that the Germans didn't intend to give us any rest and we quite made up our mind that we wouldn't give them any either. The infantry during the afternoon were driven out of Binche by sheer weight of numbers. Then developed quite a number of charges and counter-charges, which were very exciting and most interesting. We gave them all the support we could with our guns. We dealt very severely with a squadron of German cavalry who'd appeared on our right. We suddenly saw these people coming, didn't realise who they were at first and we said, 'By crikey! Its bloody Germans!' so we started gunfire immediately. We fired on open sights, fuse nought, and they got about two hundred yards from the guns and they wheeled to the left and galloped away to the left and rode right into a squadron of our own cavalry who dealt with them and finished where we'd left off.

Then quite suddenly we got the orders that we were going to try and retake Binche. This was in the early hours of the 24th. We did very well. The battle went on for several hours and I thought that we were going to take the place but I doubt very much whether we could have held it if we had. However, we were very disappointed when we were ordered to break up the battle and retreat. But we were thankful the Germans had withdrawn after this very severe battle because we were feeling thoroughly tired. We were completely exhausted, thoroughly hungry, and I don't think we were capable of any reasonable further movement. There was only one thing that kept us going and that was the knowledge that we were fighting for our very lives.[89]

89 Arthur, M., *Forgotten Voices of the Great War, Ebury Press*, London, 2003, p. 27.

After the opening skirmishes and dozens of rearguard actions, Gough received orders to change flanks. Thus began a gruelling night march. He recalled:

> *I was so sleepy that I fell asleep leaning on my horse's neck, having been up and actively employed both mentally and physically since 3.30 a.m.*[90]

Five German armies were sweeping through Belgium and were threatening to surround the British and French armies holding the Belgian front.

German infantry assaults followed artillery bombardments but they were beaten back time and time again by British rifle fire. The Salient was under attack from three sides and within hours the British casualties began mounting. With many officers killed and wounded, small pockets of British troops began a gallant stand against an enemy that outnumbered them four to one. During the evening of 23 August, Field Marshal French realised that the BEF were facing an enemy with an overwhelming superiority in manpower and weapons. If British forces did not fall back, their flanks would be left unprotected and they would be eventually overrun.

Gough and his cavalry unit would find themselves in action during the Battle of Le Cateau on 26 August 1914. II Corps were to take part in a 'holding fight'. It comprised the 3rd and 5th Divisions, with the 4th Division and Allenby's cavalry division in support. The terrain was suitable for the advancing cavalry but artillery dominated the field of battle. German artillery attempted

---

90 Gough, *Soldiering On*, p. 116.

to shell British infantry positions into submission, while German infantry attacked the flanks of the British lines. Each attack was repulsed, with the Germans suffering heavy losses. However, it was only a matter of time before the Germans managed to knock out many of the British guns. Some British soldiers managed to rescue others from the field of battle. Gough's unit found themselves separated from the cavalry division under Allenby.

After two days of severe fighting in front of Mons, Field Marshal French withdrew the British army who, along with the French army, began a retreat from the area. There were many rearguard actions that not only delayed the German advance but enabled British forces to regroup. In his memoirs, Gough recalled, '[A]nother bitter rearguard battle took place in the woods of Villers-Cotterets, and here I lost Colonel Hogg, who was killed in command of the 4th Hussars. He was the third and last of my commanding officers who had sailed from Dublin to fall thus early in the campaign.'[91]

In the confusion of war and the continual movement of troops on the field of battle, Gough contacted HQ in order to get precise orders of where his units should be. Here he spoke to Major General Henry Wilson. The old War Office official stated, 'Oh, you are on the spot. Do what you like, old boy.'[92] Though Gough was incensed at this reply he managed to extricate himself and his command and cross the River Marne to establish defensive positions.

The French army counter-attacked, stopping the advance of the German armies. Gough and his cavalry brigade expected a

---

91 Gough, *Soldiering On*, p. 117.
92 Gough, *Soldiering On*, p. 117.

German attack, and were surprised that none had materialised. He sent out a number of reconnaissance patrols who reported that there was no movement from the German positions, and on further investigation they found that the Germans had pulled out. Gough ordered his men to move forward as he galloped back to Haig's HQ. As he entered to report the German movements, he met J. E. B. Seely for the first time since their meeting at the War Office over the Curragh Incident. The officers exchanged a cold greeting.

The BEF managed to halt the German advance later that month at the Battle of the Marne, forcing the Germans to fall back to the River Aisne.

When the Germans turned to face the pursuing Allies they held one of the most strategic positions on the Western Front. The battles that followed were to have a major influence on the next four years of warfare that would scar the world. Both sides held on to the ground they had taken and on 14 September 1914, Field Marshal French ordered the BEF to dig in, marking the beginning of four years of trench warfare. German forces would hold the high ground along the River Aisne where they would launch many attacks against the Allied Forces.

Later, in the autumn of 1914, the BEF found themselves fighting in and around Ypres in Belgium.

There, the 1st Corps, under Haig, held the German turning movement on the high ground east of the town. It was a bloody struggle lasting about ten days, with the 1st Corps considerably out-numbered by the Germans. Our situation was, at times, extremely critical, but the desperate resistance of the British troops and the firm, resolute and often personal leadership of Haig and his staff, enabled our troops to hold their positions. After this opening struggle these positions of wet and muddy trenches were held with much suffering and hardships, but with resolute courage by both sides for nearly four years.[93]

This battleground would become the graveyard for the old regular British army. The men that were to follow would be part of Kitchener's volunteer army, who would also live and die in Flanders Fields.

---

93 Gough, *Soldiering On*, Arthur Baker Ltd, London, 1954, p.120.

Chapter 15

The Final Curtain

The Curragh Incident is often considered a minor affair, an episode played out in Ireland that had no effect on what was happening in the world at that time. But events at the Curragh were closely watched by the intelligence agencies of every country in Europe.

In the years that followed there would be a lot of bloodshed at home and abroad. Those that took part in the Curragh affair of 1914 continued their service to the Crown in one way or another, playing out their final acts on the world stage.

The Curragh Incident did not affect Gough's professional career as a soldier. At the outbreak of the war, Gough took his brigade to France and by September 1914 he was commanding a division. Almost two years later, in July 1916, he was commanding the 5th Army. However, before the war ended, Gough fell victim to the politicians who had failed to unseat him over the Curragh Incident when he drew most of the blame for the defeats inflicted on the 5th Army by the last major German offensive in 1918. After the war he enjoyed a successful career in business and lived to command the Home

Guard in Chelsea during World War II. His brother, John Gough, who had given so much support and advice during the Curragh Incident, was not so lucky; he was killed in February 1915 by a sniper's bullet. Like many of the other officers who were involved in the Curragh Incident, Gough penned his memoirs with specific detail to his involvement..

Major General Gerald Cuthbert remained in command of the 13th Brigade when it was mobilised for service as part of the BEF in 1914. He took the brigade to France and commanded it through the retreat from Mons, the First Battle of the Marne and the Battle of Aisne. He held various other commands throughout the war and retired from service in 1919. He died peacefully at the age of sixty-nine in 1931.

Like many other officers, Major General Sir Charles Fergusson took his division to France in 1914. He held a number of commands during the war and became military governor of Cologne until 1922. After an unsuccessful attempt to enter Parliament in 1923, he was appointed Governor General of New Zealand from 1924 to 1930. He wrote about the events at the Curragh and his involvement in his book *The Curragh Incident*. He became Chairman of the West Indies Closer Union Commission and was Lord Lieutenant of Ayrshire until his death in 1951.

Lieutenant General Arthur Paget, however, did not have much success during the war. Though Field Marshal Sir John French received the command of the BEF, he never forgot that Paget was the cause of his resignation. Because of this, French made sure that Paget never held a command during the war except a home defence one in England. After war was declared, it soon became common knowledge that Paget would not command troops in the field. On hearing this, Lady Alice Fergusson offered some words of condolence to the officer, to which Paget replied, 'Ah yes, it's a pity. I love war.' He died peacefully in 1928 aged seventy-seven.

Field Marshal Sir John French was appointed Commander-in-Chief of the BEF as it travelled to France. He clashed with a number of officers in relation to his strategy and tactics. French once again came under political pressure after the Battle of Loos and was forced to resign in 1915. He returned to England and became Commander-in-Chief of Home Forces, a post he held until the end of the war. In 1918 he was appointed Lord Lieutenant of Ireland, a post he held until his resignation in April 1921. While in this role, he sought a hard line against republicans. He survived an attempt on his life by the Irish Republican Army in 1919. French died from cancer in 1925 aged seventy-two. As one of the first of the Great War generals to die, 7,000 mourners passed his coffin as he lay in state. French's sister was Charlotte Despard, the well-known suffragette, anti-war campaigner, Irish Nationalist and Sinn Féin member.

John Redmond died a few months before the end of the war. The Easter Rising of 1916 had shattered any hopes he may have harboured of a peaceful settlement to the Irish Question.

J. E. B. Seely, who had been forced to resign as Secretary of State for War over the Curragh Incident, found himself holding the rank of major general and was in command of the Canadian Cavalry Brigade during the war. He is credited with leading the last great cavalry charge in history at the Battle of Moreuil Wood in March 1918. His exploits during the war and his revered horse 'Warrior' were captured in print and as part of a television documentary, *War Horse: The Real Story*. Seely was considered a capable and brave soldier by many. He held the title of 1st Baron Mottistone until his death at the age of seventy-nine in 1947.

Major General L. B. Friend was promoted to the post of Commander-in-Chief in Ireland in 1914. He was replaced following the Easter Rising of 1916. He received an appointment as President of the Claims Commission British Armies in France. He died in November 1944.

Winston Churchill's involvement in the Curragh Incident and Ireland's quest for Home Rule made him more enemies in a few years than most politicians make in a whole career. During the war he was demoted from his position as lord of the Admiralty over his failure to seize the Dardanelles and was subsequently forced to resign altogether over the Gallipoli campaign. His career as a politician in the early part of the twentieth century has been associated with many of Britain's military, foreign and domestic policy disasters. He would serve two terms as Conservative Prime Minister of Britain, most notably during World War II when he assumed office as Britain verged on defeat and successfully brought it to victory, and died in 1965.

The Great War was to take a great toll on the many men, both Protestant and Catholic, who answered the call for King and Country. Many of the soldiers that had been encouraged to enlist in 1914 by John Redmond, leader of the National Volunteers, found themselves in the 16th Division. Newly raised battalions from all eight Irish infantry regiments were grouped into three brigades. As part of Kitchener's Volunteers, their baptism of fire came in early 1916 and then they took part in the Somme offensive. They then fought at Messines in 1917. The division was effectively destroyed on 28 March 1918 when it was overrun during the great German offensive.

Those men who had joined the ranks of the UVF found themselves on the Western Front as part of the 36th Ulster Division fighting alongside their southern counterparts – they, too, suffered heavily on the Western Front in battles such as the Somme, Messines, Langemarck and Cambrai.

In 1915, as the crisis on the Western Front went from bad to worse, Prime Minister Asquith was forced to bring British and Irish Unionists into a coalition government. Anti-nationalists such as Bonar Law and Walter Long now had a direct say in Irish policy. A year later, in 1916, the British government changed yet again, with David Lloyd George replacing Asquith as Prime Minister with the backing of the Conservatives. The Liberal Party split as a result and the party that supported Home Rule for Ireland found itself opposing a government that was anti-Nationalist and pro-Unionist. The Great War had gradually pushed the Irish Question off the list of British government priorities.

The Curragh Incident had contributed to Unionist confidence but it had also increased Nationalist support for its own paramilitary force, the Irish Volunteers. Though the outbreak of the war effectively postponed the implementation of Home Rule, there were those who actively refused to accept this. The Easter Rising of 1916 would highlight the cause of Irish independence and encourage a new generation to take up arms against Britain. As one war ended, another one was about to begin.

Chapter 16

A Death In London

JUNE 1922

On the morning of Thursday, 22 June 1922, Unionist MP and former Chief of the Imperial General Staff Field Marshal Sir Henry Wilson sat down for breakfast at his house at 36 Eaton Place, London.

The now retired officer was once again attired in his full dress uniform and polished boots as his appointment later that day would require him to reprise his role as field marshal. He had been invited by the Chairman of the Great Eastern Railway to unveil the company's Great War memorial inside London's Liverpool Street Railway Station.

Unlike many other officers whose cards had been marked in the aftermath of the Curragh Incident, Wilson emerged unscathed. During the war he received many lucrative appointments within the army and had become a valued military adviser to Prime Minister David Lloyd George. Throughout these years he had continued to plot and scheme against the government in favour of the Ulster Unionists and the Conservatives.

However, since the end of the war, a new and uncertain age for Britain had materialised both at home and abroad. Throughout Britain's dominions, industrial action and the cause of independence had captured the headlines. Wilson found lots to object to in this changing world, from the establishment of the League of Nations, the rise of Bolshevism and the escalating situation in Ireland. Wilson believed that the increased violence brought about by such ideals should be subdued by military intervention. He was particularly concerned that the ongoing unrest in Ireland would have a knock-on effect on the colonies. He favoured imposing martial law in Ireland and the deployment of extra troops in order to suppress Irish republicans. Though he disagreed with the actions of the Black and Tans in Ireland, he once suggested that the names of Sinn Féiners should be posted on church doors and 'whenever a policeman is murdered, pick five by lot and shoot them. My view is that somehow or other terror must be met by greater terror.'[94]

As Lloyd George and his Cabinet began negotiations with Sinn Féin in 1921, Wilson's relationship with the Prime Minister rapidly deteriorated. By 1922, with his term as CIGS coming to an end, Wilson looked to the world of politics for an alternative career. With the help of his Unionist contacts, Wilson ran for election and was returned unopposed as the Unionist member for North Down.

---

94 Jeffrey, K., *Field Marshal Sir Henry Wilson*, Oxford University Press, Oxford, 2006, p. 266.

Wilson thought the truce of 11 July 1921, which brought to an end the Irish War of Independence, was 'Rank, filthy cowardice' and he hoped it would break down so that thousands of troops would be deployed in order to crush Sinn Féin. Since May of that year, Wilson had been working in Ulster advising the Northern Irish government on policing and security.

As he rose from the breakfast table on the morning of 22 June, he carefully folded his speech for the unveiling and placed it in the inside pocket of his tunic. He spent the rest of the morning browsing through the newspapers. At 11.00 hours he prepared to leave for his appointment. In the hallway he buttoned his tunic and fastened his Sam Browne belt. He attached his sword to the belt, checked himself in the mirror and twisted the ends of his moustache. Bidding farewell to his wife, he walked down his front steps to a waiting taxi.

At 13.00 hours, after a brief lunch with the railway directors, Wilson unveiled the memorial to the 1,200 railwaymen who lost their lives during the Great War.

He read his speech, quoted some relevant Kipling poetry and soon after returned by underground train to Charing Cross Station, where he got a taxi to his home in Knightsbridge.

At 14.20 hours Wilson's taxi came to a halt outside his residence. As Wilson paid the taxi driver and turned to ascend the steps to his house, two men approached him.

Unknown to Wilson, two members of the Irish Republican Army (IRA), Reginald Dunne and Joseph O' Sullivan, had been waiting for his return. As Wilson made his way up the steps to the front door, Dunne and O'Sullivan moved in on their target. The men produced two Webley Revolvers and aimed them at Wilson. Dunne later recalled:

Joe went in a straight line while I determined to intercept him [Wilson] from entering the door. Joe deliberately levelled his weapon at four yards' range and fired twice. Wilson made for the door as best he could and actually reached the doorway when I encountered him at a range of seven or eight feet. I fired three shots rapidly, the last one from the hip. I took a step forward. Wilson was now uttering short cries and in a doubled-up position staggered towards the edge of the pavement. At this point Joe fired once again and the last I saw of him he [Wilson] had collapsed.[95]

Wilson had been shot six times. In a futile attempt to defend himself, he had half withdrawn his sword from its scabbard. The dead officer lay face down on the pavement as Dunne and O'Sullivan made their escape. This attempted getaway was hindered by O'Sullivan, who had a prosthetic leg. Shouts of anger came from many passers-by as both men tried to flee. A shrill blast of a whistle announced the arrival of two constables who attempted to intercept the gunmen. Having reloaded their revolvers, both assailants turned on the police officers. A number of shots rang out and both officers collapsed on the road. A passing chauffeur tried to stop the men but he too was shot and seriously wounded. As Dunne made his getaway and O'Sullivan scuttled along behind him, the crowds of onlookers grew in number. On Ebury Street, as O'Sullivan tried to reload his weapon, the crowd surged forward and wrestled him to the ground. Dunne turned back to lend his colleague assistance but he was also apprehended. The members of the public handed

---

95 Excerpt from Dunne's official report, which was smuggled out of prison and first published in the *Sunday Press*, 14 August 1954.

the assailants over to the police, who had to protect their prisoners from a very hostile crowd.

Outside 36 Eaton Place, a large crowd of onlookers and police had assembled. Wilson's body was carried into the house and laid out on a couch in his study. Bernard Spilsbury, the famous pathologist, arrived and carried out a preliminary examination of Wilson's body. Spilsbury identified nine wounds on the body, two that would have been fatal. His official autopsy report stated:

Wilson was not shot after he had fallen. All nine wounds were inflicted when he was erect or slightly stooping, as he would be when tugging at his sword-hilt. The chest injuries were from shots fired at two different angles: one from the right to left and the other from left to right. Either would have proved fatal and produced death within ten minutes. The bullet through the right leg passed forwards and downwards, and therefore the shot came from directly behind. That in the top left shoulder had been fired from the left side and rather behind, and the downward direction proved that the arm was in a raised position as the bullet entered. The wounds in the forearms were inflicted from behind whilst the arms were still at the side of the body.

The killing of Field Marshal Wilson shocked and outraged British society. *The Times* wrote:

Field Marshal Sir Henry Wilson, the famous and gallant soldier, was murdered yesterday upon the threshold of his London home. The murderers were Irishmen. Their deed must rank among the foulest in the foul category of Irish political crimes.[96]

---

96 *The Times*, 23 June 1922.

On investigation, both assailants were discovered to be London-based IRA volunteers. Dunne had served with the Irish Guards during the war. O'Sullivan had also served in the British army and had lost his leg at Ypres.

The revolvers used by the assassins were sent to Lloyd George and Winston Churchill in the Cabinet Room of 10 Downing Street. Churchill later wrote, 'There was no Henry Wilson. The Prime Minister and I faced each other, and on the table between us lay the pistols which an hour before had taken this loyal man's life.'[97]

At the inquest on 26 June, the taxi driver said that he had seen only one gunman who had fired at Wilson from a range of about three yards. Another witness, a road mender who was working outside 36 Eaton Place, testified as follows:

He saw Sir Henry Wilson get out of the taxi-cab. Sir Henry took a pace across the pavement when witness heard a report. Sir Henry completed the distance across the pavement and had just got his foot on the first step when there was another shot. Sir Henry attempted to put the key in the door when there was more firing. Sir Henry bent down as through to avoid more shots. There was more firing, and witness saw the Field Marshal fall across the pavement, his head on the kerb. Witness saw a big man with a revolver standing on the kerb about three yards from the General.

Witness said he saw the man actually fire once. He saw a smaller man also with a revolver directly behind the taxi-cab. He would be about four yards from Sir Henry.

---

97 Langworth, *Churchill in His Own Words*, p. 761.

The Coroner – So that actually there was one man on each side of the Field Marshal, about three or four yards from him? Yes.

Witness said he saw both men fire several shots.[98]

As to be expected, Wilson's funeral was a very public affair and was attended by Prime Minister Lloyd George and the Cabinet. Wilson's widow, Cecil Mary Wilson, blamed the government for her husband's death and was only persuaded to allow government representation at the funeral because it would be considered disrespectful to refuse the King. Many of the Field Marshal's former military colleagues from at home and abroad attended the ceremony.

Wilson was buried in the crypt of St Paul's Cathedral. *The Times* praised Wilson as a 'Warrior Irishman' being laid to rest 'between two gallant Irishmen, Lord Roberts and Lord Wolseley'. However the *New Statesman* claimed that because of Wilson's devotion to 'force and force alone' he was the British counterpart to Irish republican Cathal Brugha.

On 2 July 1922, Dunne and O'Sullivan were tried together at the Old Bailey before Mr Justice Shearman. Both men claimed that they had not set out to kill Wilson. On hearing of the unveiling ceremony at Liverpool Street Station, both men had reconnoitred the station but found that the area of the unveiling would be closed to the general public. They decided to go to Wilson's house and had not planned to kill him. The shooting happened in the heat of the moment.[99] There had been no escape plan and, with O'Sullivan only having one leg,

98 Jeffrey, *Field Marshal Sir Henry Wilson*, p. 282.
99 Jeffrey, *Field Marshal Sir Henry Wilson*, p. 283.

their withdrawal from the scene of the shooting would have been almost impossible without a vehicle.

On cross examination, Dunne stated that during the Great War he had been 'fighting for the principles for which this country [England] stood. Those principles I found as an Irishman were not applied to my own country...'. Dunne requested that he be allowed read a prepared statement from the dock. This request was refused. However, the speech was smuggled out of prison and printed in the *Irish Independent* on 21 July 1922. In it Dunne wrote that he blamed Wilson for the 'Orange Terror' as he was the military adviser to the Belfast government who had raised the Ulster Special Constabulary. He continued:

> *We took our part in supporting the aspirations of our fellow coun-trymen in the same way as we took our part in supporting the nations of the world who fought for the rights of small nation-alities.... The same principles for which we shed our blood on the battle-field of Europe led us to commit the act we are charged with.*

> *You can condemn us to death today, but you cannot deprive us of the belief that what we have done is necessary to preserve the lives and happiness of our countrymen in Ireland. You may, by your verdict, find us guilty, but we will go to the scaffold justified by the verdict of our own consciences.*

After three minutes of deliberation, both O'Sullivan and Dunne were found guilty of murder and sentenced to death. In Ireland, the Chairman of the Provisional Government in Ireland, Michael Collins, ordered that an escape plan be formed in order to rescue the two men. While members of the IRA deliberated over a possible scheme, civil war erupted in Ireland and the planned rescue was shelved. After an unsuccessful appeal, both men were hanged together in a double execution on 10 August 1922, at London's Wandsworth Prison. Their bodies were interred within the prison grounds. In 1967 their bodies were repatriated to Ireland and buried in Deansgrange Cemetery.

Seven months before Wilson's assassination, on 6 December 1921, the Anglo-Irish Treaty had been signed between an Irish delegation, led by Michael Collins, and the British government. This Treaty had been approved by the Dáil in early January 1922 by a small majority. Arthur Griffith and Michael Collins formed a pro-Treaty provisional government, while Eamon De Valera and others who objected to the Treaty withdrew from the Dáil. In Dublin an armed standoff commenced between pro- and anti-Treaty forces. The latter occupied the Four Courts in April 1922.

In Ireland, as in Britain, rumours abounded as to who had ordered the hit on Wilson. Many believed that the republican movement in Ireland had ordered and arranged the Field Marshal's demise. Had the killers acted alone or was there a more sinister plot afoot? Did Michael Collins sanction the killing or was it ordered by the anti-Treaty forces that were holed up in the Four Courts in Dublin?

As mentioned, Dunne and O'Sullivan had both fought in the British army during the war. Both men subsequently became active members of the London section of the IRA. While they claimed to have acted alone in their killing of Wilson and that their reason for the killing was in protest to

Wilson's involvement in the pogroms against the Catholic population that were being unleashed in the north of Ireland, it is possible that their resentment against Wilson may have come from their service during the war. Having enlisted to fight for the rights of small nationalities, one of the leaders that they had followed was now implementing a similar programme of terror against their countrymen. Whether this was a personal vendetta against Wilson or part of a republican plan, it is difficult to determine the thoughts that went through the minds of Dunne and O'Sullivan as they pulled the triggers.

The British government believed that Wilson's assassins were acting on orders from the Irish Republican Army Executive and that those within the Four Courts were responsible for his death. Winston Churchill wrote to Collins threatening that unless Free State troops moved against the anti-Treaty forces, the British government would take control of the situation and deploy troops against the anti-Treatyites. Those within the courts disavowed any knowledge of the mission to kill Wilson.

On 28 June 1922, Free State artillery unleashed a salvo against the Four Courts. In a matter of days, Dublin City was burning. Wilson's death and Michael Collins' act of aggression against his former comrades had precipitated one of the greatest tragedies in Irish history, that of civil war.

Chapter 17

A Victory For
The Military

'Any army,' wrote Richard Watt, 'is a flicker away from becoming an armed gang. The only thing that prevents this is military discipline, which is an incredibly flimsy institution, if its subjects but knew it.'[100]

The maintenance of discipline in the British army was always considered a very serious affair.

All soldiers swore an oath of allegiance to the King.

I [name] swear by almighty God, that I will be faithful and bear true allegiance to his Majesty, King George the Fifth, his heirs and successors, and that I will, as in duty bound, honestly and faithfully defend his Majesty, his heirs and successors in person, crown and dignity against all enemies, and will observe and obey all orders of His Majesty, his heirs and successors, and of generals and officers set over me. So help me God.[101]

---

100   Watt, R., *Dare Call it Treason*, Dorset Books, London, 1964, p. 107.
101   *The Soldier*, December 1957, p. 37.

By 1914, after almost a century of worldwide conflict, the British army had established a reputation as a highly motivated armed force that was willing to serve King, Queen and country without hesitation. Amongst the ranks of soldiers and officers there was an unequivocal commitment, self-sacrifice and mutual trust. The British army looked to its tradition of excellence that was reflected in its standards of professionalism amongst the ranks. It was this quality that engendered the support of the public in its many campaigns of the nineteenth century.

The Curragh Incident was the greatest threat to government rule in Britain since the English Civil War in 1642. The army, the House of Lords, the Conservative opposition and the King had all conspired to defeat the democratically elected government. Senior officers backed by influential politicians had not only challenged the government but had argued the fact publicly, undermining the legitimacy of government rule in England.

Often incorrectly described as mutineers, Gough and his colonels were not guilty of mutiny as they did not disobey any direct orders. The definition of a mutiny given in the *Manual of Military Law* was:

Mutiny implies collective insubordination, or a combination of two or more persons to resist or to induce others to resist lawful military authority.[102]

Major General Fergusson stated that the Curragh Incident was a classic case of confusion caused by muddled motives and

---

102   General Despatch No. 105 op. cit. p74, L/MIL/7/13314.

inadequate orders.[103] It is difficult to believe that the failure to pass on an order could cause so many disharmonies and almost cause a civil war amongst those sworn to uphold an allegiance to the King.

The incident poisoned civil-military relations and also those relationships within the officer corps on the eve of the Great War. Events were fuelled by politicians and army personnel. In relation to Sir Henry Wilson's involvement in the Curragh Incident, the historian A. P. Ryan wrote:

His unabashed incessant habit of playing politics while holding high rank in the Service was an inexcusable exhibition of disloyalty. The titbits of information he carried, as proudly as a dog with a shopping basket in its mouth, to the opposition leaders were useful to them in their campaigning against the Government.[104]

This misconception of the events at the Curragh in 1914 contributed to a vendetta against the armed forces by the government. Both sides remained suspicious of one another as mobilisation for war in Europe was taking place. Many in the army believed that such mobilisation was for possible war in Ireland and, though orders were obeyed, a lack of trust between the government and army was evident.

There are a number of questions that arise in relation to the Curragh Incident. Perhaps the most frequently asked is why did such an incident take place? The Curragh affair is often used by historians as an example of the political involvement of

103   Fergusson, *The Curragh Incident.*
104   Ryan, *Mutiny at the Curragh*, p. 102.

Britian's military in the Ulster crisis as it is often assumed that many of those officers serving in Irish regiments were Anglo-Irish. It is an interesting fact that, while there were many such officers in the ranks, Gough's 5th Lancers, who were an Irish cavalry regiment and directly involved in the incident, only had five officers out of twenty-eight who were registered as being Anglo-Irish.[105]

Recent research reveals that the Protestant Ascendancy did not dominate the ranks of the British army in Ireland as many historians have assumed.

This of course does not contradict the likelihood that many officers had relatives in Ulster, but the low percentage of Anglo-Irish in the regiment makes the chance of connections in Ulster less than if the regiment had been heavily officered with Anglo-Irish. Figures were not available for the other cavalry regiments involved in the Curragh crisis; but since the Lancers were an Irish regiment, one can safely assume that its Anglo-Irish proportion was at least comparable to other regiments.[106]

The idea that the Curragh Incident was part of a plot to coerce Ulster to accept Home Rule and that the corridors of Whitehall abounded with conspiracy continued to titillate those who sought answers to the behaviour of the military. Adjutant General Ewart, writing later, laid the blame for the rumours of a plot firmly on Paget.

---

105   History of the 5th Irish Lancers, MS 8000, National Army Museum, London, 1924, p. 200.

106   Muenger, *The British Military Dilemma in Ireland 1886–1914*, p. 164-203.

Several things puzzled me about the whole business. I absolutely repudiated, and repudiate, the legend which was so assiduously put about, that there had been a wicked conspiracy to coerce Ulster or to provoke Ulster to take the initiative. Nothing was said in my presence which could have been so interpreted.... Yet at the same time I could not understand why Paget was not removed from his command, and I could not help asking myself whether, unknown to myself, something had been said to him, or some instruction given to him, of which I knew nothing.... If Paget said half the things attributed to him [in the papers] he must have been, if not a lunatic, a tactless idiot, unfit to command anywhere.

Others believed that the plans to move troops to Ulster had been known for a considerable length of time. In his memoirs, Gough alleged Sir Henry Wilson was aware all along of the government's plans for the invasion of Ulster but did nothing 'until the gaff was blown', so to speak, by the resignations at the Curragh. As a result of this, Gough's brother John refused to speak to Wilson again.[107]

As Britain prepared for war in Europe, the government knew it had to be careful in its mobilisation plans as any mistakes with orders could lead to another incident where the military would refuse to move.

The outnumbered British Expeditionary Force that found itself in France and Belgium during August of 1914 managed to halt the advancing German and Austro-Hungarian forces, enabling a line of defence to be established. Though the army suffered heavy casualties, they proved that they were willing to fight and obey orders from the civil administration. At the

---

107   Gough, *Soldiering On*, p. 171.

outbreak of the war, the British government had regained its control over its army and it was this important factor that would enable it to not only stop the German advance but also to continue fighting around the world for the next four years. A new army had to be raised and the government needed to control this army so that it would fight anywhere it was needed. While there were some minor incidents of disobedience in the forces during the war, the government never saw a repeat of the Curragh Incident.

The British army's involvement in the Ulster crisis and the British government's failure to act appropriately left a deep distrust among Irish Nationalists. There is no doubt that the outbreak of war in Europe in 1914 diffused the situation in Ireland at that time. However, unknown to most, there was a Nationalist plan to rebel against British rule in Ireland, which would manifest itself in the form of the Easter Rising of April 1916.

Conclusion

Though the Curragh Incident was not technically a mutiny, as no orders were given or disobeyed, the results seriously damaged the relationship between the British government and its army on the eve of the Great War. The British army fought with great tenacity during those autumnal months at the beginning of the war and for many their duty would cost them their lives. The thousands of war memorials are testament to that sacrifice.

The political melodrama played out between Westminster, Belfast and the plains of the Curragh in County Kildare greatly increased the confidence of Ulster Unionists.

The Great War had averted a civil war in Ireland in 1914, but for Irish Nationalists the events that had unfolded during the early months of that year confirmed their doubts about Prime Minister Asquith's real commitment to granting Home Rule for Ireland. The 1916 Easter Rising, the guerrilla war that followed and the devastation brought about by Ireland's civil war were just the beginning of decades of violence in Ireland, north and south of a border that partitioned the country.

Just before Christmas 1914, all ranks of the 3rd Cavalry Brigade that had been stationed at the Curragh received a

Christmas card from the people of Ulster. The verse inscribed read:

One hundred Noble Officers, of England's pride today,
Have stood upon the Curragh Camp a summons to obey,
Their General said, 'I've orders that to Ulster you must go,
And there shoot down their loyal men, as you would a foreign foe,
The Government of England, in the hands of roguish knaves,
Give orders, spite of conscience, you must this Home Rule save,
For we're pledged to John Redmond them to Roman bondage drag,
Their only crime, we must confess, is loyalty to the flag.'

Chorus
But it is a famous story, proclaim it far and near
Of this noble band, One Hundred, who stood for honour dear,
And refused to go to Ulster, their rights to take away,
Or be a party to this plan to give John Redmond sway.
General Paget gave the order; cried Gough, 'Can it be true?
Are we to shoot down loyal men? Why this we cannot do.
We remember, Sir, when England stood in danger grave,
These very men have shed their blood our noble flag to save,
You may order us to Russia, or to the mouth of hell,
But we'll never go to Ulster and enslave those loyal men,
We're loyal, Sir, to England, until the end of time,
But before we'll coerce Ulster our command we will resign.[108]

Unknown to many of those who sent these Christmas cards to the Curragh Camp in December 1914, many of the officers

---

108 Beckett, *The Army and the Curragh Incident 1914*, p. 385.

and men of the 3rd Cavalry Brigade had already been killed or wounded at the battles of the Marne, the Aisne and Ypres during the autumn of that year.

Many of those officers who had stood firm and defied the British government in March 1914 would never return to Britain or Ireland. Killed in action, their final resting place was far from home in France and Belgium. Those who survived the war would return to a country that was undergoing dramatic changes.

As the question of Home Rule for Ireland once again came to the fore, nationalists in Ireland and throughout many of Britain's colonies began a campaign for independence that would stretch the British army and the government to its limits. It was the beginning of the end for the British Empire.

Edward Carson (Kilmainham Gaol)

General Hubert Gough
(Brian Curragh)

Sir Arthur Paget
(Brian Curragh)

Curragh Camp Cavalry Barracks 1914 (Author's collection)

Appendix

THE IRISH COMMAND IN 1914

Major General in charge of Administration
Major General L. B. Friend

General Officer Commanding, Parkgate, Dublin
Lieutenant General Sir Arthur Paget

General Staff
BGGS Brigadier General G. T. Forestier Walker

Major General in charge   Major General L. B. Friend
   of Administration

Administrative, technical and departmental staff

3rd Cavalry Brigade, Curragh
Brigadier General H. P. Gough

4th Hussars, Curragh	III Brigade, RHA, Newbridge
5th Lancers, Dublin	4 Fd Troop, RE, Curragh
16th Lancers, Curragh	3 Signal Troop, RE, Curragh

5th Division, Curragh
Major General Sir Charles Fergusson

13th Infantry Brigade, Dublin
Brigadier General G. J. Cuthbert

2 KOSB	1 RWK
2 West Riding	2 KOYLI

14th Infantry Brigade, Curragh
Brigadier General S. P. Rolt

2 Suffolks

1 East Surreys (Dublin)

1 DCLI

2 Manchesters

15th Infantry Brigade, Belfast
Brigadier General Count Gleichen

1 Norfolks (Holywood)

1 Beds (Mullingar)

1 Cheshire (Londonderry)

I Dorsets (Belfast)

Divisional Artillery
Brigadier General J. E. W. Headlam

VIII (Howitzer) Brigade, RFA	Kildare	37, 61, 65 batteries
XV Brigade, RFA	Kildare	11, 52, 80 batteries
XXVII Brigade, RFA	Newbridge	119, 120, 121 batteries
XXV111 Brigade, RFA	Dundalk	122, 123, 124 batteries

Divisional Engineers
7 Fd Co., RE	Curragh
59 Fd Co., RE	Curragh
5 Signal Co., RE	Curragh

6th Division, Cork
Major General W. P. Pulteney

16th Infantry Brigade, Fermoy
Brigadier General E. C. Ingouville-Williams

1 East Kent (Fermoy)

1 Leicesters (Fermoy)

1 SLI (Tipperary)

2 York and Lancaster (Limerick)

17th Infantry Brigade, Cork
Brigadier General W. R. B. Doran

1 Royal Fusiliers (Kinsale)

1 North Staffs (Buttevant)

2 Leinsters (Cork)

3 Rifle Brigade (Cork)

Divisional Artillery, Mallow
Brigadier General W. L. H. Paget

XII (Howitzer) Brigade, RFA	Fethard, Clonmel, Kilkenny	
	43, 86, 87 batteries	
II Brigade, RFA	Cahir	21, 42, 53 batteries
XXIV Brigade, RFA	Ballincollig	110, 111, 112 batteries
XXXVIII Brigade, RFA	Fermoy	
Divisional Engineers	Waterford	24, 34, 72 batteries
12 Fd Co., RE	Moore Park	
38 Fd Co., RE	Cork	
6 Signal Co., RE	Limerick	

Defended Ports
North Irish Coastal Defences – Lough Swilly and Belfast
South Irish Coastal Defences – Queenstown Harbour and Berehaven

No. 11 District
Colonel F. F. Hill
No. 12 District
Colonel S. W. Scrace-Dickins

Index